Ah, the humble LEGO. A simple plastic brick. Made of pure acrylonitrile-butadiene-styrene. Hollow on one side and studded on the other. Multicolored. The brightest possible greens and reds and blues. From an obscure factory in Denmark. From a random assemblage of LEGO, one can build most anything—a pirate ship, a star cruiser, fake teeth, even a working toaster oven! (Okay, maybe I lied about the last two.)

When I was a child, LEGO were the little plastic keys to another universe. A universe of engineered imagination. For the 5- to 10-year-old little Rainn, those tiny, snappy bricks occupied hundreds of hours of my life. And do I want those hours back? No, sir. That was time spent in peaceful, quiet creativity, building LEGO on the knotty canvas of the '70s deep-pile carpet of our 1,000-square-foot rental house in suburban Seattle. (I'm convinced there are still some 2x2 bricks lost to eternity in that polyester shag!) The artistic line that was drawn from a (literal) shoebox full of little cubes, bricks, planks, and blocks to their eventual formation into a race car, or spaceship, or phantasmagorical house was a magical one. I'll never forget those countless tiny moments of specific realizations that led to a mind-blowing build: "Oooohhh, if I snap this little doohickey on the opposite side of this element, I can match it on the other side, creating a symmetrical look and feel, and snap a plate underneath, like THAT! *(snaps plate)*, then I can create the longest, most *swooshable* flying laser gun known to man!"

And what is *swooshable*, you might ask? Well, it's a real, technical term: the kinetic, palpable ability of something you've built to *SWOOSH* through the air in a supercool way, sparking the imagination and inspiration. (As well as sparking whatever gun/jet/swooshing/afterburner sounds you can make out of the side of your mouth.)

And now? I'm an adult and, sadly, not much in my life is *swooshable* anymore. However, I have a really cool job. I get paid to pretend to be other people. How amazing is that?! From one world of pretend to another. Every once in a while, I pinch myself and think, "What a ridiculous way to make a living!!!"

Here's another ridiculous (AND *swooshable*) way to make a living. Get people to pay you to play with LEGO! Just like Adam Ward. Adam is a LEGO artist, magician, and creativity guru. Now, there are a lot of LEGO builders out there on the inter-webs and the YouTubes. Assembling Star Wars kits in a time-lapse video; showing you how to make a castle with real, working catapults; unboxing a new LEGO set, fresh from the factory in Denmark; etc. But what Adam does is extraordinary. He builds LEGO with heart. With soul. His creations inspire and uplift!

Adam can build life-size rainbow unicorns WITHOUT INSTRUCTIONS. He just looks at a pile of LEGO, and like a master builder from *The LEGO Movie*, the parts fuse together conceptually in his brain. He can build signs using a custom LEGO alphabet. And he makes *useful* things out of LEGO, too. Not just rocket ships and miniature Ferris wheels. But picture frames. iPhone cases. Coasters. Key docks. (I need to talk to him about getting one of those. My keys never seem to be where I know I just put them.)

Over 10 years ago, I started the media company SoulPancake with some friends. It was a forum to create inspiring media content for young people. We wanted to connect humans. Uplift them. Give viewers a vision for a loving, noble future for humanity, but do it via pure ENTERTAINMENT! And when we added Adam to our roster, we knew we had found someone truly special. Adam is the definition of SoulPancake-y. He works hard to find joy and light in every day. He is a master of the well-timed dad joke. He even leads device-free retreats into the wilderness for adults because he believes meaningful human connection matters. And SoulPancake is a human connection company! Match. Made. Mind. Blown.

And the fans responded. More than 8 million views across 24 episodes. LEGO nerds, art nerds, regular nerds have united to make *Brick x Brick* one of our most beloved series. And now? The show has become a book! Take it with you everywhere! Show it off! Leave it on your (LEGO) coffee table. Give it to your niece who wants to use LEGO to soar into other dimensions! Buy 175 of these books and use them to make a tree house in your backyard! Just use your imagination. And your heart.

And so, I leave you with this here book—lovingly constructed with Adam's taste, style, humor, and vision, as well as his radically beautiful builds. There are also some fan favorites from our *Brick x Brick* YouTube series in its pages! It's a celebration of LEGO as a tool for creating something beautiful and soul-felt. Something that is still super-duper cool but has some greater meaning in the world. Because this is what we do at SoulPancake—we try to make the commonplace magical, spark conversation, connect through creativity, and, above all, make life more *SWOOSHABLE*!!!

"This book hereby has my **unofficial official** stamp of **approval**."

Rainn Wilson

Welcome, friends! I'm **glad** you're here.

Now let's answer some questions! **Three questions**, to be exact!

QUESTION #1: WHO IS ADAM WARD?

I am! I am a LEGO-loving (duh!) "grown-up" who has been playing with LEGO since I was 2 years old. So, like, a very long time, because I'm way older than that now.

When I was **2**, my family moved from an old house in Minneapolis to a slightly less old house in Minneapolis. When we went to look at a potential new house, the kid who lived there at the time lived in the room that would eventually become my room. He was very cool, and he was probably **7** or **8** at the time. When we toured the house, we arrived at his room, and he had SO MUCH LEGO! He had all of the loose bricks just dumped out on the floor of his (soon to be my) closet. I remember seeing all that LEGO and thinking, "WHAT IS THIS MAGIC?!?"

I let my dad cut my hair once. Once.

Mom, please hold all questions 'til the end.

Now, I know my parents didn't choose that house based solely on the fact that the bedroom closet held a lot of LEGO. But the fact that my incredibly curious, loud, half-Jewish, afro-sporting, 2-year-old self didn't bother them at all during the entire duration of the house tour almost certainly gave them the time and space to learn more about that house than any others we toured. The very fact that toddler me, cold chillin', playing with LEGO that belonged to some kid I didn't even know is directly responsible for the house I grew up in is bananas!

My parents were concerned with trivialities like how many bathrooms the place had, the school district, square footage, etc. I was only concerned with one thing: "Do these magic blocks come with the house?" Spoiler alert: They did not. Total bummer, I know! But my parents saw my fascination with LEGO. And soon, that house would be ours, that room would be mine, and that closet floor would be covered by my own magic bricks.

This event also served as my introduction to LEGO. An introduction that would very quickly become an obsession, and an obsession

My dad has never looked cooler, and I would 1 million percent still rock pink pants.

Purifying myself in the waters of Lake Minnetonka.

that would grow and grow, and eventually lead me to transform my favorite toy of all time (sorry, Ninja Turtles, Super Soakers, and Nerf jousting swords) into a career.

All I wanted to do growing up was build with LEGO . . . and get my hands on even more LEGO. **Every birthday. Every holiday.** All I asked for was LEGO. Every trip to the store: **"Can we please just look at LEGO?"** Every garage sale: "Maybe they have some LEGO!"

LEGO can wear a little dude out.

This room had the highest **dad-jokes** per capita in the universe.

to need my help. I briefly turned my attention away from LEGO to the adventures of Donatello, Leonardo, Raph, and Mike. Time away from LEGO is totally normal.

Now I admit, there was a short period of time when the crime-fighting reptiles who skateboarded and devoured pizza beneath the streets of New York City seemed

Santa, I'd like one Futuron Monorail set, please. Also, what's a Victorian **Christmas?**

Bar Mitzvah vibes. Also, this 13-year-old "man" is a full head shorter than his 5' 3" **mom**.

came time to draw it, it just looked like a weird, sad horse with a party hat on its nose. I'd imagine making elaborate bridges and structures with Play-Doh, but they'd fall over and come apart and make my hands smell weird. Not only did LEGO never give me stinky hands, it also very rarely let me down. I knew how to build strong things that could stand up to the rigors of play. I could dream something up, build it, save it, add to it, change it, update it, incorporate new pieces as I found them, and make my builds cooler and cooler. All of these factors deepened my love for the mighty brick.

But LEGO would always draw me back. As a kid, I got very good at LEGO. And you may be wondering what I even mean by "good." Does that mean I could follow the directions well or connect the pieces easily? Yes . . . and more. What I mean is that I could imagine something I wanted to build, take some time, and actually bring it into existence. This becomes incredibly important later, as this ability to create what I wanted to didn't really translate to any other artistic medium. For example, I could think of cool things to draw, like a robot rhinoceros with a rocket horn, but when it

Consider yourself lucky this book has **no sound.**

Not to toot my own horn, but I also entered a LEGO contest as a kid and did QUITE well. It was for a Disney movie you've probably never heard of, *The Rocketeer*. They held a LEGO rocket-building contest in preparation for the movie's release, and I entered, taking it very seriously. I used an absurd amount of LEGO. I scrounged for hours for all the pieces I needed. In the end, I built a super colorful rocket slightly taller than I was. It had everything: jet thrusters, laser cannons, multiple docking bays, cockpits, satellites. It was probably the most impressive thing I had ever built. My parents helped me load it into our Dodge Caravan and brought it to the movie theater to display. I felt pretty good about my chances . . . until I realized it wasn't only kids that had entered this contest.

The University of Minnesota engineering department had built a rocket that I think later actually went to space. Some WEIRDO

Ah, a simpler time, when trolls were on cakes and not **message boards.**

grown-up who was SO OLD (like 25 years old) also entered a rocket. I got third place. My parents were proud, though reasonably upset that their kid was competing against college students and random adults. But I was thrilled. I won a Rocketeer lunchbox, the Rocketeer Nintendo game, and like 400 Rocketeer pins. Well, I *was* happy . . . until I learned that the top prize was a trip to Disney World, and about like $1,000, which was basically infinity dollars to an 8-year-old. So, I decided to retire from LEGO contests and take a nearly 20-year break from the brick.

My journey back to LEGO began in December 2010. It was a fateful night. I think it actually may have been an afternoon. Nope, it was morning. Definitely morning. Fateful morning.

That doesn't really have the same ring to it . . . it was just a morning.

My awesome roomie, Vinnie, had just upgraded our TV situation. He bought a sweet new flat-screen, a surround-sound system, a Nintendo Wii, an Apple TV—the whole shebang. I helped him set everything up, and we binge-watched movies and played video games like we had never seen a screen before.

TVs actually used to look like this.

During one of our unhealthily long sessions, the movie just stopped. Panic set in. *Please don't let it be something wrong with the world's heaviest television!*

We switched inputs. Phew! The Wii was still working. We could still play *Wii Sports Home Run Derby* for 9 straight hours. The problem must be the Apple TV. I reached into the little cubby where the Apple TV lived, and pulled it out. The box was crazy hot. Uhh . . . that's not great.

Apparently, it had overheated and shut down. I guess being in a "top-bunk" situation with an audio receiver isn't the ideal home for an Apple TV. Gets too hot up there to function.

Our setup was so cool; we couldn't change it! So like every infomercial ever, I thought, "There's gotta be a better way!" If we could just raise the Apple TV a few inches off the receiver to keep it cool, we'd be all set. This became my mission. So, like countless determined people before me, I went to the Mecca of all things . . . Target.

I figured surely they'd have some little shelf-y thing that would help me save the day.

They did not. Yes, Target was failing me. But as I was leaving Target, I happened down the LEGO aisle, where I said a bunch of very 2010-y stuff.

"Oh awesome—new Star Wars sets. Man, those prequels were bad . . . I wonder if they'll ever make more?"

"Harry Potter castle? That's sweet. I gotta read those books! I'm not too old, right?"

Then I stopped cold in my tracks. It was as if that tiny bolt of lightning on Harry's forehead had jumped off and struck mine. How could I have been so blind?!? The solution was painfully obvious. Duh, times a million.

BUILD THE SHELF OUT OF LEGO!!!

See? Target never fails.

I sprinted to my car and zoomed home *Fast and the Furious*–style. Thankfully, it was only 12 blocks. I often imagine what would have happened had I been pulled over.

"WHY YOU'RE CERTAINLY IN A HURRY, YOUNG MAN. WHAT'S THE RUSH?"—POLICE OFFICER

"SORRY, SIR! IT'S AN EMERGENCY! I'M ON MY WAY TO BUILD A LEGO SHELF FOR MY APPLE TV THAT'S BEEN OVERHEATING. OUR NEW TV IS TOO HEAVY TO MOVE, SO WE CAN'T CHANGE THE CORD, AND I GOTTA PROTECT MY BACK SO I CAN KICK MY ROOMMATE'S BUTT AT *WII SPORTS HOME RUN DERBY*. I CAN'T NOT FIX IT! I CAN'T!"—LUNATIC DRIVER, AKA ME

I would have 100% been thrown in jail.

Fortunately, I made it home safely. I burst open a bin of dusty old LEGO and built like a madman. Turns out building with LEGO is like riding a bike.

The shelf fit the Apple TV perfectly, and the Apple TV never overheated again.

In most stories, that would be the happy ending. But for me, building this little shelf awakened a dormant part of myself. Suddenly, all I wanted to do was build. And play a liiiiitle bit of *Wii Sports*.

Prior to that moment, I had never thought of LEGO as anything but a toy. For the first time, I made something useful for my home. It served a purpose. And I began to see LEGO as a tool, and eventually as a medium.

I quickly became hooked. My bedroom was a semi-converted one-car garage furnished with a hodgepodge of super cheapo Craigslist furniture and curbside freebies, so there was **lots** of room for improvement. Now I could make my room rock. I had LEGO.

I designed and built a hutch for my cheap desk, which instantly made it look about **500** times cooler. WHOOP! I used to lose my keys ALL. THE. TIME. So, I built a little key fob and dock to park my keys by my door whenever I got home. WHAM! No more overpriced locksmiths. I had a bunch of photos in a shoebox under my bed, so I built a bunch of picture frames to cover my semi-painted white walls. BAM! I built a side table next to my bed, and when I got sick of my phone falling off it at night, I built a little

You know you're cool when your clothes color coordinate with the floor.

stand for it. BOOM! I was notorious for my drinks ruining coffee tables, so I made some super sleek coasters to replace the cardboard circles we swiped from sports bars. SWOOSH!

I low-key felt like I had a superpower. I felt like I could literally make whatever I needed, whatever I wanted from LEGO. But like all superheroes . . .

YES, I JUST REFERRED TO MYSELF AS A SUPERHERO. THIS IS MY BOOK, SO I CAN TOTALLY DO THAT. WHEN YOU WRITE A BOOK, YOU CAN CALL YOURSELF WHATEVER YOU LIKE. AND I WILL HIGH-FIVE YOU, AND ABSOLUTELY CALL YOU THAT NAME, MC SEÑOR RADICAL NINJA MASTER. NOW, WHERE WAS I?

So like all superheroes . . . MYSELF INCLUDED, THANK YOU VERY MUCH . . . I had a weakness. I had a limited supply of LEGO bricks, and I was running out.

So I sat down to brainstorm what my next business venture would be to help me generate some income to buy bricks, and I realized the answer was staring me in the face.

BUILD THE BUSINESS OUT OF LEGO!!!

Um, I mean . . .

BUILD A BUSINESS BUILDING THINGS OUT OF LEGO!!!

Duh, times a million and one.

Turning a wall into a giant **LEGO postcard**... you know, working.

In hindsight, it seems painfully obvious, but at the time, it felt like a ludicrous idea. I mean, how was I going to get people to *pay me to play with LEGO?*

Obviously, I take my job VERY seriously. I'm wearing 4 tuxedos as I type this.

That would be my business. I would build everyday stuff out of LEGO for people who loved LEGO when they were younger. Things like picture frames, key chains, lamps, piggy banks, jewelry boxes, and so on. And hopefully, people would buy them!

I decided to launch a Kickstarter campaign to start my company in February 2012. I needed money to buy bricks, and I needed customers to sell to. I thought if I played it just right, maybe I could get both.

I thought a lot about it. I thought about how every kid I knew when I was little loved LEGO. It didn't matter if they were cool or nerdy or sporty or obsessed with the Muppets; they all built things. But I only knew of a few adults who still built with LEGO, and they were all niche fans, like lovers of Star Wars or people who built model trains. There didn't seem to be LEGO products for regular non-super fans.

Balloons are the best, and this one won't fly away!

It worked! I exceeded my goal and got my business off the ground. In the years since, my art studio, Peace + Bricks, has grown and grown. I've been able to work with some amazing people and companies, and I've built thousands of pieces using millions of bricks that are now all over the globe.

I've built little stuff, big stuff, ridiculous stuff, and all sorts of stuff in between. I got to work on some of the LEGO movies; I have had pieces displayed in museums; I set a world record—all thanks to LEGO. I also created and host the YouTube series *Brick x Brick* that inspired the book I'm writing now! And actually, by the time you are reading this, there will be some other very cool LEGO-y things happening. It's a **brick-citing time to be alive!**

One of my first LEGO art shows!

LEGO ART EXHIBIT

LEGO ART EXHIBIT

QUESTION #2: WHY IS LEGO IMPORTANT?

I've been building with LEGO for practically my whole life. And there are a ton of reasons why LEGO is awesome and cool and fun. But I also think LEGO is an **important** toy for kids and grown-ups to play with.

First, they are analog. Meaning, they aren't on a screen. Don't get me wrong. I love my screens. I'm in front of one right now. The very existence of this book is largely due to my occasional existence on your screens. But it is still so so so so so (that's five so's) important that we continue to do things in the real world. My daughter, Plum, is 1. (Well, she will be 2 by the time you read this. Actually, she could be like 11, or 39, or 84, if you found this in a used bookstore in the future. Whoa.) Anyway, she basically lives a screen-free life, and I am infinitely jealous of her. Not only because she gets nearly 200 minutes of naptime every day, but because she doesn't HAVE to be on screens yet. Most grown-ups HAVE to be on a screen a bunch of hours every day, but that doesn't mean that kids have to. It's nice that there are still some things we can do off-screen.

-End of rant-

But not the end of why I think LEGO is important. Here are more reasons:

As a kid, I was able to use playing with LEGO to channel my creativity constructively. It has helped me profoundly as a creator. LEGO supported the growth of my imagination as I created characters, built worlds, and told stories with bricks.

LEGO helped me develop some more left-brain skills, too. To this day, I am an excellent amateur grocery bagger, trunk loader, and suitcase packer. I think all of these skills developed in part due to my constant planning, designing, building, and rebuilding with LEGO. All that building also majorly supported my math and problem-solving skills.

To be clear, I'm not claiming that playing with LEGO will magically make you good at math or become more creative. I believe that creativity and math abilities were already in me, but LEGO certainly supported these skills by supplying me with real-world scenarios to navigate, and they might help you too! When we build, we're voluntarily, and excitedly, crunching numbers to figure out how many **4x4** plates we need to cover the entire ninja hideout, or how long a brontosaurus tail we can build with the pieces we have. These lessons stick.

LEGO also supported my self-confidence. This may sound strange, but think about it for a moment (you can then go back to thinking about how otters hold hands). Practically every time you sit down to build a new LEGO set, right in front of you is something you *can't* do, or at least haven't ever done before. And a few minutes, or hours, or maybe even days later, BOOM! You have done that thing. All of these instances of transforming *I can't*'s into *I just did*'s! added up to make me believe that I could do practically anything, even make a living playing with bricks.

QUESTION #3: WHAT IS BRICK X BRICK? OR, WHAT IS THIS SHOW ON THIS THING CALLED YOUTUBE?

Brick x Brick is a nontraditional how-to LEGO series that I created with the awesome media company SoulPancake that I also host! You can watch it on SoulPancake's YouTube channel or Amazon Prime, and select episodes are on the LEGO Life app. On it, we strive to bring you fun new LEGO builds that can also make a difference and spread joy in your community, family, and life.

If you've never heard of SoulPancake, it's a content company cofounded by Rainn Wilson, a really cool actor and funny dude who also wrote the foreword to this book. Their mission is to make stuff that matters, which they've been doing for more than a decade now. They create wonderful, positive content to inspire us, give us hope, and encourage us to ask life's big questions. I think they care about LEGO for

Observe the web series host in his natural habitat.

many of the same reasons I do. LEGO can be an empowering tool that connects us, and they're all about connection. LEGO has the power to enable us to make wildly fun, weird things that never existed before, and they love doing that, too! I mean they're pretty darn lovable. So, when I was thinking about making a show around LEGO, SoulPancake was obviously the best collaborative partner in the multiverse. I mean, there is this one company in Universe PW51 that is actually run by minifigs and where it rains cookies, but they didn't have bubbly water on tap or a joyful company culture.

We were a match made in LEGO heaven. And in the years we have been working together, we've made a bunch of episodes, racked up millions of views, and have connected with thousands of people who, like you, also love LEGO. Now, we're working together to bring you this book. And who knows what comes next?! Rock concerts with LEGO instruments? Sending LEGO spaceships to the moon? Designer LEGO sneakers that can order a pizza? Okay, probably none of those things, but other equally cool things to come. **Stay tuned!**

Talkin' LEGO with strangers on the street for the show is the BEST!

HOW TO USE THIS BOOK

Okay, okay, okay. I know you know how to use a book. I mean, obviously you're a **super smart, awesome person** because you're currently holding this book, which means you rock to the maximum.

Me trying to figure out the new LEGO VIP points system.

But it turns out books can be used in a multitude of ways. When I was 8, I made this amazing pillow fort—out of pillows, not LEGO, but you just gave me an idea! The left side of my fort sagged a bit, so I scavenged my house for a solution. I had recently received a fifteen-volume children's encyclopedia full of terrific info on dinosaurs, space, the ocean, and more. Now remember, this was *before* the internet. We couldn't just ask a shiny cylinder in our kitchen who invented the mustache. We had to go to a library to find a dusty old book on facial hair history. (I sound a million years old.) Anyway, I used six of these heavy (and apparently expensive) books to prop up the fort and level out my cushiony hideaway. My mom was the opposite of stoked about this. To this day, whenever she gives me a present, she brings it up. When my daughter was born, she gave me a blanket from when I was a baby. First words out of her mouth: "Please don't use this in a fort."

Regardless of what anyone says, you can 100% use this book in a fort. But if you're looking to use it to support your journey as a builder, these 5 tips will help.

1. **DON'T WORRY ABOUT MATCHING MY BUILDS OR MY PIECES 100%.** This book is all about *improvising* and making the coolest, most fun thing possible out of the bricks you DO have, not just stressing about the bricks you don't. Plus, I'm sure you have a birthday, or a holiday, or a stellar report card coming up. So when folks ask what you want for said gift-giving event, tell them: *"Mas LEGO por favor!"*

2. **FEEL FREE TO SKIP AROUND, JUMP AHEAD, OR JUST OPEN UP TO A RANDOM PAGE.** You needn't go in order. You don't have to build the first build first. Heck, you don't even have to build the first build at all! If you're already a whiz at helicopters, then skip mine! This isn't *The History of Facial Hair*. This is meant to be a super fun read. So grab some bricks, pick a page at random, and start making magic.

3. **MAKE THIS BOOK MESSY.** This book is also not a collector's item. Okay, maybe one day it will be, so buy two, and keep one in your book safe. You do have a book safe, right? Good. So, for your non-book-safe version, I encourage you to dog-ear pages, write in it, take notes, circle things, underline and highlight stuff you like, and add your own jokes! Hopefully, some stuff in this book makes you go, "No way!" Or, "I never knew that!" Or, "That's amazing!" Or, "Who's Freddie?!?" When you come across something like that, make a note, because maybe it'll help you with future builds, and I want you to be able to find it super quickly and easily. Also, Freddie is my imaginary ocelot sidekick . . . and the name of a really cool robot you will build later.

4. **SHARE WHATEVER YOU'RE BUILDING!** You're not Tony Stark in a cave at the beginning of *Iron Man*, so don't keep what you're working on a secret! Please please please share your builds with the world! Even if you're not interested in (or allowed to go on) social media, *no problemo*. Share your builds IRL. Bring your builds to a friend's house, family gathering, or to show and tell (if that's still a thing). Sharing what you're working on is a great way to connect with people, get new ideas, and inspire them to make stuff, too!

5. **TAKE YOUR TIME, AND BE PREPARED TO MESS UP.** Some builds and processes in this book will be new to you, and they may be challenging. That is ALL GOOD. This is not a race. If a build is taking longer than you expected, all that means is you are learning more than you thought you would. That is a great thing! If your build isn't turning out how you wanted, you can tinker with it, or just take the whole thing apart and start over. That's one of the things that is so great about LEGO. I restart builds all the time—it's just a part of the process. Sometimes it's frustrating, and sometimes I get mad and shout a bunch of gibberish at my cat, but eventually I come back to the bricks and build my way out.

<< A SPECIAL NOTE FOR THE GROWN-UPS >>

No build in this book will require more than approximately 100 pieces. My goal here isn't to make elaborate, intricate, over-the-top, uber-complicated builds that your amazing kid can never re-create again without this book in hand. My goal is to help your budding builder explore new techniques, build new skills, foster their own creativity, and unlock new possibilities. Then they can go on to bring their own out-of-the-LEGO-box ideas to life! So let them experiment and mix things up. Because while following the rules is important, this is a book where there are no real rules. Just kids who rule! And grown-ups who rule, too. Seriously, you rule! I just checked.

Professor Wardington's Super Scientific Difficulty Level Rating System

EASY PEASY.

Of course you can build this. I know, I know! You could probably build these blindfolded, with your hands behind your back, and on one foot. But just because these builds are easy doesn't mean they're not awesome. Cereal is one of the easiest meals to make in the history of meals to make, but are you gonna tell me cereal isn't amazing?!? Yeah, of course you're not, because you're basically a genius, and as all geniuses know, cereal is terrific.

YOU GOT THIS!

You'll probably have to remove the blindfold, but you got this, champ. These builds might incorporate some smaller parts that require attention to detail and fine motor skills. These builds may also require intermediate building techniques and have slightly higher piece counts than the previous level.

CHALLENGE ACCEPTED.

Now we're talking! At last a challenge. I mean, it's not like the world's most challenging of challenges, but at least we're in the vicinity of difficult.

UM . . . WHAT NOW?

Wait. Huh? Ohhh . . . I see what you're doing here! Yeah, these builds may cause you to take a pause here and there, until you get the hang of it. You still got it, but you may need to slooooooooow doooooooown to ensure all the parts are finding their proper homes in the builds. These builds will also likely utilize some techniques, parts, and sequences you may be unfamiliar with.

APPROACHING DEFCON.

Adam, what are you doing to us?!? I thought we were friends, man. I know these builds may seem a little bonkers, but I promise, you can do it! These builds will absolutely incorporate some elements and techniques you've never even heard of. But how cool is that? You get to pick up some new tricks along the way. Don't hesitate to ask someone for help for these builds.

Six Degrees of Fragility

And fragility was in Footloose with Kevin Bacon!

POKE WITH PILLOW, EXPLODES.

These builds are lovely to look at, but don't stare, as the intensity of you not blinking may cause them to disintegrate into a pile of bricks and regret. Also, try not to exhale too powerfully.

BELONGS IN YOUR GRANDMA'S GLASS CABINET.

You can gently handle these builds, to demonstrate their coolness, but please do so with caution, and don't let your cousin Tucker hold it. You know how Tucker can be.

BUILT FOR PLAY.

These builds are built to be used. So use them! Play with them, let them help you in your daily adventures, and let them make your life a teensy bit better. They likely have some weak points though, so just be aware. If someone doesn't know how to use them, or handle LEGO in general, you'll likely have some fixes to make. Maybe let Tucker play with these, but keep an eye on that little rascal.

JUST DON'T DO KARATE ON IT.

Hold 'em, pick 'em up, let your friends have turns with 'em, just don't get super roughhouse-y. If these builds get dropped, or kicked, or drop-kicked, you'll likely have to do some repairs, but you fortunately won't be playing 52 brick-up, which is not a great game.

ONCE FOUGHT A BEAR, BUT LOST.

These builds will stand up to the toughest use and interaction. Still, don't drop it off your roof for funsies. Also, get off your roof! You're not Santa. Or if you are Santa, hi! I hope you like all the cookies I've left you over the years, and thanks again for that Super Nintendo back in 1992. You're the best!

HIT WITH BAT, REPLACE BAT.

Don't worry about breaking these builds. I told them to be careful handling you.

The Brickabulary

Building with LEGO is like learning to speak Parseltongue. (Do you learn Parseltongue, or do you just magically know it? Really must read Harry Potter.) LEGO requires learning a whole lot of new words. LEGO has its own language, vocabulary, and techniques.

So, to help you along, I present to you **THE BRICKABULARY**—the ultimate vocabulary guide to every brick, technique, and cool insider LEGO lexicon you will need to know in order to use this book. It's kind of like a glossary, but way easier to read. It starts on page **210**.

Naming Pieces

Let's name him after your great-granddad, Fredbrick.

BUT . . . before you look up the difference between bricks and plates and tiles, it is super duper helpful to understand HOW to name parts of different sizes. Whether you're building with friends, looking for parts online, or following the directions in this book, understanding this will help big-time.

Most builders will use phrases like **"2 by 8 brick"** or **"4 by 4 plate"** or **"1 by 6 tile."** But what exactly do they mean?

Here's a simple way to think about it. Almost all LEGO pieces are rectangles. Yes, even the squares. (Squares are also rectangles. #geometry) They generally have 4 sides, with at least 2 of the sides being the same length. When a piece is described as a **"2 by 4,"** that means the short sides have 2 studs, and the long sides have 4 studs. A **"1 by 8"** would be a long, skinny piece with only a single row of 8 studs. This method of naming is used for almost all LEGO parts,

bricks, plates, tiles, and more. Also, when writing, people normally use the letter **x** to replace *by*, so **2x8**, **4x4**, **1x6**, etc. Pro tip: If the two numbers are the same—such as a **1x1** or **2x2** or **4x4** or **6x6**—then the part it's referring to is a square part.

It can be helpful to count the studs on each side until you get the hang of it. Also, remember that LEGO loves even numbers, so aside from **1x1s**, **1x3's**, **2x3's**, and the occasional **3x3's**, there are almost no other parts with an odd number of studs. There is no such thing as a **2x5** or **1x7** or **4x13**.

Every once in a while, you'll see a piece that is taller than your average LEGO brick. When we're naming these pieces, we add a third number to indicate the height. If there's a **1x2** brick that is twice as tall as a normal 1x2 brick, we call it a **"1x2x2."** If it's 5 times as tall, we call it a **"1x2x5."** Make sense? Woohoo! If it doesn't, no sweat. Maybe try reading it again. **Or have a snack. Everything makes more sense with snacks.**

Just a few more points, I promise.

If the piece is a **"tile"** or **"jumper"** or **"modified"** part (more on these terms in **"The Brickabulary"**), things get a teensy bit confusing. Instead of counting the studs, we name the piece in terms of how much space it would take up IF it had studs. For example, a **1x8** tile has zero studs, but it is the same shape as a **1x8** brick, and it takes up the same amount of space. Even though it has zero studs, it's not a **0x0**—it's still called a **1x8**. With rounded parts, treat them as squares and just put the word **rounded** in front of them— rounded **1x1**, rounded **4x4**, etc.

Some pieces have very complicated names. Like **"inverted 4x6 wedge with open studs . . . yada yada yada."** In these cases, just describe the piece. Those ultra weirdo pieces are used really infrequently. So don't stress it.

LEGO also has a part number associated with each piece, which can be helpful for ordering parts online, but it's 0% necessary for building or using this book. Also, the LEGO part number has no relationship to the type of piece. If you say **2x3** brick, you can kind of figure out what the piece is by hearing the name. But say **"LEGO part #3795,"** and I'd never be able to guess that is a **2x6** plate. Would you? I have not yet learned the mysteries of official brick naming. Maybe one day . . . maybe one day.

Fun fact! In the LEGO Movie universe, when characters are master building, the part number kinda flashes above the pieces right before they use them to create their masterpieces. If that happens to you while you're building, you may be an animated LEGO character! Lucky.

Micro Challenge Time!

1. Go to the **Brickabulary**.

2. Look up the term *minifig* and read the description.

3. Pat yourself on the back. **You learned something!**

4. Now gather up all the minifigs you have and Frankenstein together the **WEIRDEST** combo possible. I'm talkin' pilot torso, wizard cape, evening-gown legs, and pirate face with a cowboy hat . . . on roller skates . . . holding a hot dog . . . and a Batarang. Niiiiiiice.

At last! A pizza mechanic for scuba-diving ballerinas.

5. Take a selfie with your minifig-enstein and post it online tagged with **#brickxbrick**. I can't wait to see your masterpieces.

THE BUILDER AGREEMENT

I, the incredible, brilliant, talented, and magical

hereby agree to abide by the following agreements whilst using this book:

I PROMISE to not take anything in here too seriously. This is not the SATs or a Buzzfeed *Which Muppet Are You?* quiz, so I don't have to stress the results.

I PROMISE to be kind to myself. Whatever happens is perfect. Even if I feel frustration bubbling up like a poorly poured soda, I shall remember that I am trying something new, that I am awesome, and even the frustration is part of it.

I PROMISE to take a break if the frustration feels like too much, and I promise not to ever throw this book across the room like Adam Ward did with the Monopoly game board when he thought his babysitter was cheating (she 100% was, by the way).

I PROMISE to show my builds to at least one other person. When sharing my builds, I accept that this other person may not "get" my vision and may see something different than I see. This is okay! It does not make them wrong. It does not make me wrong. It just makes us individuals.

I PROMISE not to turn this book into a competition. It is not a race. It is not a build-off. It is not even a checklist. It is just a fun little guide here to support you.

Above all, I promise to have fun, to try my best,
and to enjoy this journey we're on together.

Please check one:

⬤ **I AM NOT A ROBOT.**   ⬤ **I AM A ROBOT.**

Signature: _____   Date: _____

PART 1

STUFF THAT'S ALIVE

THE PLANT

The Orchid

The first time somebody asked me if I could build them a flower out of LEGO, I felt silly. I didn't feel silly because it was an odd request, or because I had a weird shirt on that I thought fit but must have shrunk in the dryer. I felt silly because I had somehow never considered building a flower out of LEGO. Who am I? It took a friend of a friend having a super random birthday present request for me to start building flowers.

Now that I build them, I LOVE building them. I've always felt positively about flowers. I enjoy smelling them when I see them out in the world, and I think they're generally terrific creations. Thanks, nature.

We rarely see them in LEGO, though, aside from the little 1x1 plate with the stems, or a similar little piece here and there. And that's part of what makes building them so fun. People aren't expecting to see them. And as creators and artists, when we can play with people's expectations, some really fun stuff happens. Also, there are so many different varieties of wildflowers out there, you can really do whatever you want and nobody will say, "No flower looks like that!" And if someone does say that to you, just give them a hug because they obviously need one.

Who needs a bow tie when you can sport a LEGO flower on your lapel!

Good news! You can never overwater this guy. →

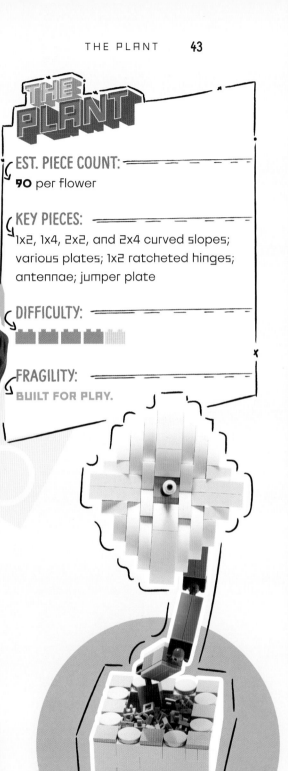

THE PLANT

EST. PIECE COUNT:
90 per flower

KEY PIECES:
1x2, 1x4, 2x2, and 2x4 curved slopes; various plates; 1x2 ratcheted hinges; antennae; jumper plate

DIFFICULTY:

FRAGILITY:
BUILT FOR PLAY.

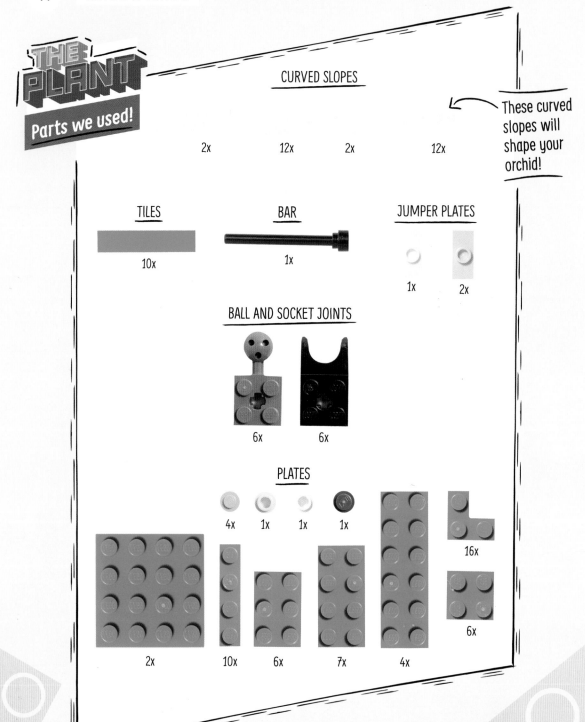

THE PLANT
Parts we used!

CURVED SLOPES

These curved slopes will shape your orchid!

2x   12x   2x   12x

TILES
10x

BAR
1x

JUMPER PLATES
1x   2x

BALL AND SOCKET JOINTS
6x   6x

PLATES
4x   1x   1x   1x   16x

2x   10x   6x   7x   4x   6x

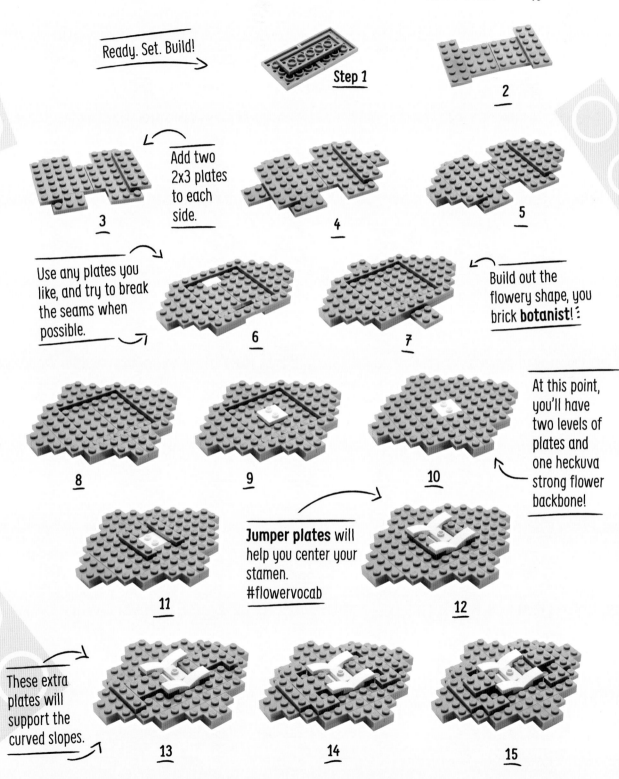

Ready. Set. Build!

Step 1

2

Add two 2x3 plates to each side.

3

4

5

Use any plates you like, and try to break the seams when possible.

6

7

Build out the flowery shape, you brick **botanist**!

8

9

10

At this point, you'll have two levels of plates and one heckuva strong flower backbone!

Jumper plates will help you center your stamen. #flowervocab

11

12

These extra plates will support the curved slopes.

13

14

15

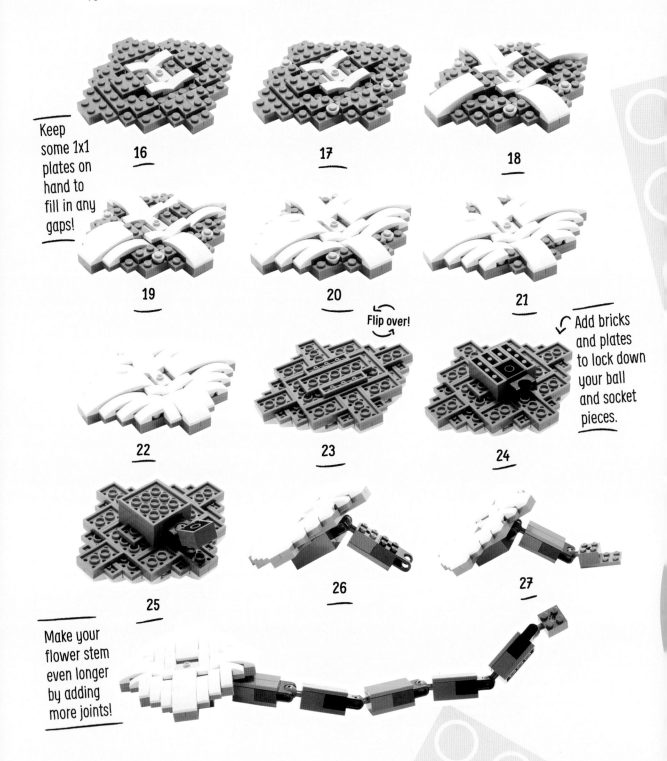

Keep some 1x1 plates on hand to fill in any gaps!

16

17

18

19

20

21

Flip over!

22

23

Add bricks and plates to lock down your ball and socket pieces.

24

25

26

27

Make your flower stem even longer by adding more joints!

Make a basic planter with loose bricks. Remember to break those seams!

Your Pick-a-Brick cup can double as a vase! ⟶ Fill the bottom with whatever little pieces you have.

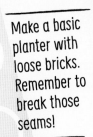

Now that's a plant you can't kill!

REMIX IT UP

Of course, you can build these in any color you like, and as you start feeling more comfortable building flowers, you can start arranging bouquets of your favorite ones, mixing and matching types and styles. They're way easier to care for than living ones, and they never wilt, or if they do, you can just reinforce the build. Also, you can play with presentation. Want them in a vase? A planter? Loose like they were freshly cut? Still a stem in the ground? You can do any and all!

Strange But True LEGO Facts

(I promise, or at least I think these things are true. You have the internet. Feel free to fact-check me.)

LEGO is a **Danish** company that gets its name from the Danish words *leg godt*, which means "play well."

LEGO was founded by **a carpenter** who originally produced wooden toys.

LEGO is the **world's largest tire manufacturer,** by number of tires produced.

There are over **915 million** ways to combine six **2x4 bricks.** To give you an idea of what a bananas big number that is, consider this: If you were to build every single combo, taking only six seconds each time (which is pretty darn fast), and you built 24 hours a day, 365 days a year, it would take you 174 years.

The LEGO build with **the highest piece** count ever (so far) was created in 2016. It was an advertisement for Land Rover, and the build reproduced London's Tower Bridge. The total number **of bricks** used was 5,805,846. The build beat the previous record holder, which was an enormous Star Wars X-wing Starfighter, which was made up of **only** 5,335,200 bricks.

LEGO bricks are produced at a massive, fully automated scale, meaning most parts are only ever handled **by robots**, conveyor belts, and machines before being boxed up. So when you open a LEGO set, you are very likely the first person on earth to ever touch those pieces!

LEGO first started making plastic bricks in **1949**. While there have been significant improvements in the construction, your pieces today would still be able to connect to bricks that are more than 60 years old.

There are over **4 billion** minifigs on the planet. If they were a country, they'd easily have the world's largest population, and they'd even have a higher population than the 6 largest countries combined.

THE REPTILE

The Sssssssnakelet

This slithery serpentine spy slides onto the scene super smoothly and sneakily, slyly in secrecy. Shh . . . if I blow her cover, she won't even speak to me.

The Snakelet can be a snake, lizard, or bracelet! You can easily add arms, legs, or other appendages as you please. When you're done going on your Snake-peditions, you can easily wrap her around your wrist by connecting the ball joint in her mouth to the socket joint at the end of her tail. Then hit the town! Have fun out there, buckaroo.

THE REPTILE

EST. PIECE COUNT:

79 (snake form) // **150** (fully lizard-ed out)

KEY PIECES:

Ball-and-socket joint plates, 1x2x4 brackets, boat tiles, modified 1x1 plate with clip light, 5x2 bracket

DIFFICULTY:

FRAGILITY:

JUST DON'T DO KARATE ON IT.

THE REPTILE
Parts we used!

BRACKETS

2x

1x

2x

PLATES

12x

4x

4x

TILES

2x

CLAWS/TEETH

4x

2x

MODIFIED PLATES

2x

BALL AND SOCKET JOINTS

5x

5x

BOAT TILES

6x

CLIPS & BARS

1x

1x

SLOPES

2x

24x

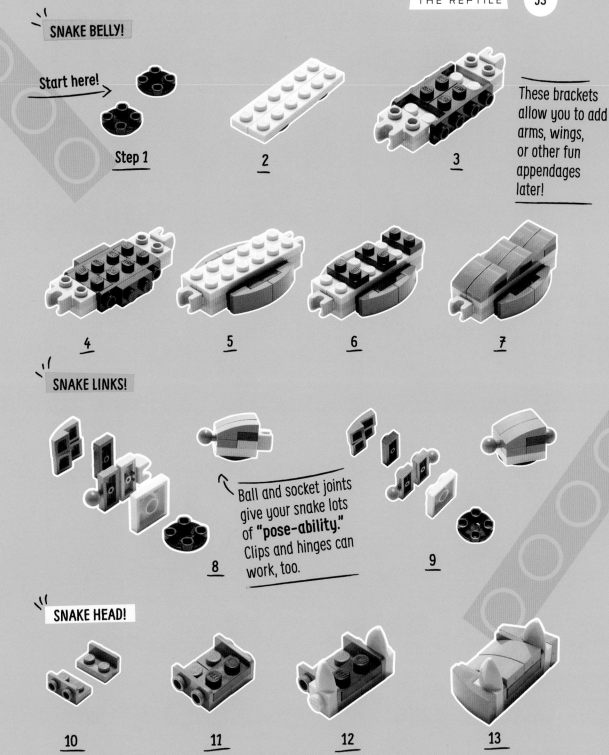

SNAKE BELLY!

Start here! → Step 1

2

3

These brackets allow you to add arms, wings, or other fun appendages later!

4

5

6

7

SNAKE LINKS!

Ball and socket joints give your snake lots of **"pose-ability."** Clips and hinges can work, too.

8

9

SNAKE HEAD!

10

11

12

13

Teeth everywhere!

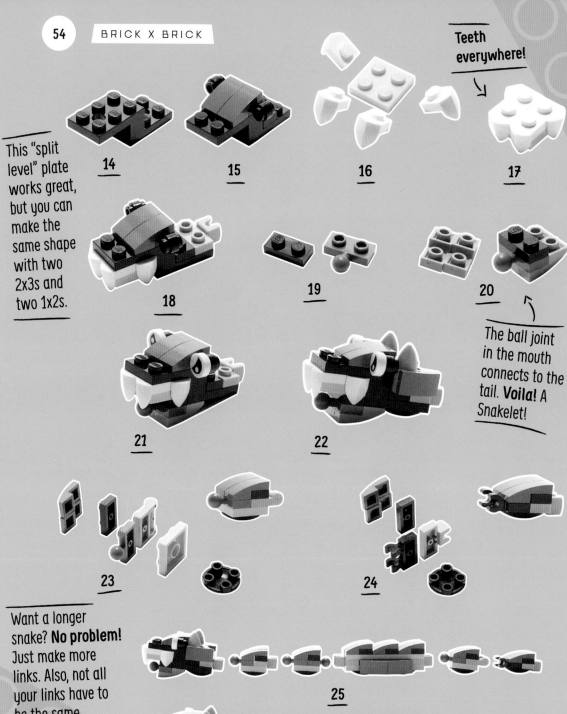

14

15

16

17

This "split level" plate works great, but you can make the same shape with two 2x3s and two 1x2s.

18

19

20

21

22

The ball joint in the mouth connects to the tail. **Voila!** A Snakelet!

23

24

Want a longer snake? **No problem!** Just make more links. Also, not all your links have to be the same. As they say: Get creative! Get, get creative!

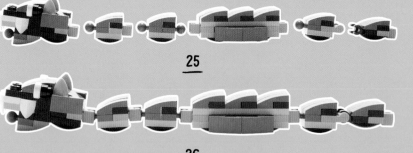

25

26

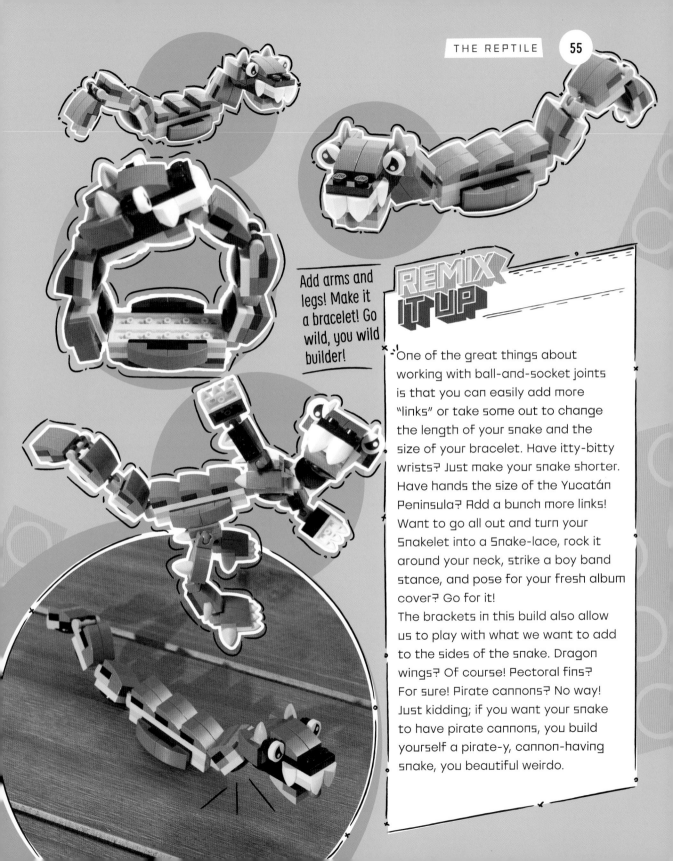

Add arms and legs! Make it a bracelet! Go wild, you wild builder!

REMIX IT UP

One of the great things about working with ball-and-socket joints is that you can easily add more "links" or take some out to change the length of your snake and the size of your bracelet. Have itty-bitty wrists? Just make your snake shorter. Have hands the size of the Yucatán Peninsula? Add a bunch more links! Want to go all out and turn your Snakelet into a Snake-lace, rock it around your neck, strike a boy band stance, and pose for your fresh album cover? Go for it!

The brackets in this build also allow us to play with what we want to add to the sides of the snake. Dragon wings? Of course! Pectoral fins? For sure! Pirate cannons? No way! Just kidding; if you want your snake to have pirate cannons, you build yourself a pirate-y, cannon-having snake, you beautiful weirdo.

The 10 Most Awesome and Generally Super Useful Pieces

1x1 SNOT Brick (4 studs, 2 studs, 1 stud)

These parts help you *change directions*. Changing directions in a build is a wonderful way to add complexity. It can also help you achieve certain effects that you would otherwise have a very hard time accomplishing. These come in super-duper handy when making spherical shapes and other rounded weirdness. They also provide the perfect place to pop a couple eyeballs and immediately bring life to your build.

1x2 Modified Ball-and-Socket Joint Plates

Speaking of bringing life to your builds, these magical little parts make the list. Nothing makes your build look more alive faster than the ball and socket joints. Wanna know why? Because most living things have actual ball and socket joints inside their bodies! No, I don't mean most living creatures have eaten LEGO. I mean that if you think of a land-dwelling animal, odds are, somewhere in their physiology, there is a ball and socket joint.

1x2 Clip and Bar Plates

If the ball and socket joint plates are the gold medal in bringing life to your builds, then these elements make their country super proud by bringing home the silver. These can do more than make your build come alive, though. These parts are also great for building modular structures that you want to be able to disconnect and rearrange. You can use them to build diagonally between adjoining levels of a build. You can create dynamic angles by using many of them. They come in tons of styles and orientations, all of which have their own specialty, so it's great to have a few of each type around.

4x4 Plate

This piece may seem like an odd choice for this list, as it's just a simple square, but it is highly useful. The 4x4 is the smallest "large format plate." By "large format," I mean a plate where both numbers are larger than 2. These parts are a great central, or starting, place for a build. Drop some axle plates on the sides and boom, you've got yourself the base of a vehicle. If you have four 1x plates, you can place one on every corner, sandwich another 4x4 on top, and bam, you have a little creature or person. If you have 6 of these pieces and some SNOT bricks or brackets, you can easily make a cube. See? I told you. Highly. Useful.

2x2 Turntable Plate

DJ BRICKY SAINT JAMES IN THE HOUSE!!! (SIREN SOUND X3!!!) Oh, is that not the type of turntable we're talking about? Ohhhh, I see. THAT kind. Phew. It was about to get crazy up in here, y'all. A good soundtrack to your builds is ESSENTIAL, so we *could* be talking about that kind, but we're talking about this kind. *These* turntables allow for smooth rotation, and the 2x2 turntable plate is the best (and easiest) way to bring magical movement to your builds. You can do it with other parts, too, but if you've got these, they make your life much easier.

1x2 Jumper Plate

Want to center a piece in the middle of a 1x2? Want to go from 2 studs to 3 studs? Want to have a smaller gap between posts or columns or other vertical elements of your build? Well, my ambitious builder bud, this is the part for you. I heart the jumper plate because it allows you to move a half stud. If you're building at a small scale or just trying to pack a lot of detail into a tight area, this part will be your bestie.

2x2 Corner Plate

I always want to call these parts a 1x2 corner brick, because they feel more like a 1x2 wrapping around a corner, but LEGO, and people who know way more than me, call them 2x2, so I guess I'll play along. These pieces are sweeeeeeeet. They are indispensable when working on technical builds, spherical structures, reinforcing tight spaces, and more. They're a bit like duct tape, and just like duct tape, you'll rarely come across a building problem these nifty right-angled fellows cannot help fix. Not doing the trick? Just use more 2x2 corner plates.

1x8 Brick

"Another snoozer," you say? Well, to that I say, "Nay!" This unassuming log-lookin' LEGO has saved my keister more times than I can count, and I am a very good counter. When building at a larger scale, it's necessary to reinforce sections constantly. These pieces are long enough to do that beautifully. Need to "break a seam" to add some strength to your creation? The 1x8 has got your back.

48x48 Baseplate

This, the largest single piece in the LEGO family, is also one of my favorites. And believe me, I don't just like it because it's gigantic. I'm not interested in "the world's biggest sandwich" if it tastes like cardboard, socks, and black licorice. I want it to actually be delicious! And this piece is delicious . . . constructionally speaking. This piece is like a huge blank canvas. It's the blinking vertical line in the top left corner of a blank Word document just waiting to be populated with your story. I love this piece because of the possibilities it contains. When I bust one of these out, I almost always have a moment of awe and intimidation. It really is a huge piece. A few moments into building, I realize, not only can I fill this up, but I'm thinking about grabbing another one.

Brick Separator

Perhaps my fave piece of all time, the brick separator is a must-have for any serious, semi-serious, super serious, or never-in-their-goofy-joke-filled-life-been-serious builder. This part will save your fingernails, your teeth, and your sanity. The brick separator is just that. It's the piece that helps you take apart pieces that you didn't mean to connect or parts that you connected long ago, and it's time to decouple. It works very well. Its only shortcoming is when it is tasked with removing two identical pieces from on top of each other. In this case it's beneficial to have two brick separators working together to remove the stubborn twin bricks. The pin on top also helps dislodge tricky little Technic elements, and you can even get SUPER creative and use it in builds. Just make sure you have a spare one for when it comes time to take that build apart.

I LOVE YOU!

THE MAMMAL

Mammalus Brickius to the Maximus

Observe the *Mammalus Brickius to the Maximus* in its natural habitat. Long thought to be endangered, extinct, or possibly imaginary, the *Mammalus Brickius to the Maximus—* or "MBM" for short—has recently been spotted numerous times in and around Denmark and cool people's houses all over the world. A peaceful, quiet creature, the MBM has no known predators or prey. In fact, it is unknown what, if anything, the MBM actually eats. According to legend, the MBM descends from a proud lineage of pre-brick-storic mammals.

What I love about the MBMs is how expressive and pose-able they are.

You can tilt their heads up, down, or side to side, and position it at many angles. You can even give them that famous "puzzled dog" look. I love that look. My dog, Maple, unsurprisingly gives me that look all the time because (spoiler alert!) I do weird things! You can articulate the limbs and tail and have your MBM strike all types of poses. Your MBM can basically do yoga. If you ever wanted to create a stop-motion video, the MBM would absolutely make an amazing costar.

THE MAMMAL

EST. PIECE COUNT:
77

KEY PIECES:
Brackets, modified 1x2 with clips on end, curved slopes, and ball-and-socket joint plates

DIFFICULTY:

FRAGILITY:
JUST DON'T DO KARATE ON IT.

THE MAMMAL
Parts we used!

SPECIALTY PIECES

2X

TILES

7X

PLATES

1x

4X

1x

1x

1X

BALL AND SOCKET JOINTS

1X   1X

SLOPES

24x

4x

CLIPS & BARS

5X   10X   4X   1X

BRACKETS

3X   1X   2X   2X

BRICKS

1X

FOR PLUM . . .

and all the other kids (and former kids)

who still see the "wowwwww" in the world.

TABLE OF CONTENTS

FOREWORD

by Rainn Wilson

Bears. Beets.
LEGO Battlestar
Galactica.

THE BODY!

Start here!

Step 1

2

3

These brackets help you build in all directions.

4

5

6

Curved slopes will help your build go from boxy to **"mammally."**

7

Make those **arms!**

8

9

10

The left and right arms are mirrors of each other!

11

12

13

THE HEAD!

14

15

16

17

Who you callin' mammal head? →

18

19

20

21

22

23

Time to shake your tail!

24

25

26

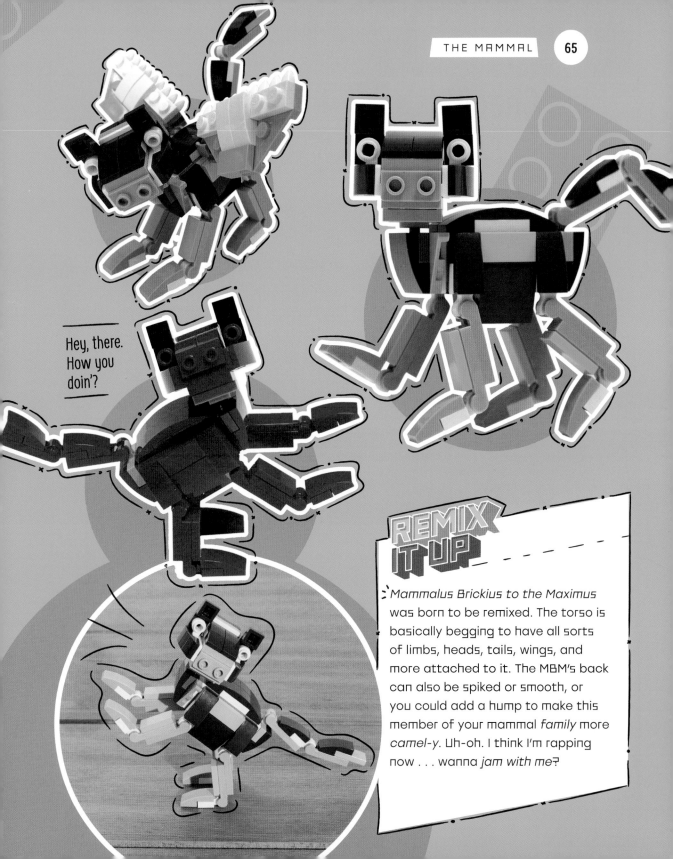

Hey, there. How you doin'?

REMIX IT UP

Mammalus Brickius to the Maximus was born to be remixed. The torso is basically begging to have all sorts of limbs, heads, tails, wings, and more attached to it. The MBM's back can also be spiked or smooth, or you could add a hump to make this member of your mammal *family* more *camel-y*. Uh-oh. I think I'm rapping now . . . wanna *jam with me*?

It's Cheap! It's Free!
The Best Ways to Get Cheap, or Even FREE, LEGO!

Ask around! Someone you know may be sitting on a big ol' pile of LEGO (hopefully not literally). They may have some forgotten bricks they want to get rid of, so you'd actually be doing them a favor. Talk about a win/win. So don't be shy, McFly! Ask your family, your friends, your neighbors, your dog sitter, your dental hygienist, your vice principal, your co-workers. And of course, be sure to ask your friend's neighbor's dog sitter's dental hygienist's vice principal's co-workers. They may just have some bricks for ya, too!

Scour yard sales. Peep Saturday morning yard sales and online yard-sale-type places like Craigslist. Sometimes, you can find some real sweet deals! It's always good to check to make sure you're buying actual LEGO, though. Sometimes people sell a bag or box of bricks "by the pound," but when you peek inside the container, it's got a bunch of weird stuff mixed in. I've found erasers, cereal box toys, knock-off LEGO, old batteries, pennies, Pogs, and other trinkets in many a box that was supposedly 100% LEGO.

Go to BrickLink.com. It's like the eBay of LEGO. If you're looking for one weirdo piece, or a whole set that was retired before you were even born, it's on BrickLink.com. Sometimes you can find amazing deals, but you can always find what you're looking for. BrickLink is a community of millions of users and tens of thousands of stores all selling LEGO. It's pretty mind-blowing, and it's a wonderful resource.

Join a LEGO Users Group. These LUGs are all over, so check for one in your area. You can join up with them for many cool activities, builds, and events. Sometimes they do set swaps, brick giveaways, and other fun LEGO-getting activities. This is a great place to meet other brick fans in your 'hood as well!

Go to the LEGO Store! If your city has one, amazing. And even if your city doesn't have one, next time you go on a vacation or road trip, check to see if there is one where you're going. The LEGO Store has one of my favorite walls in the history of walls, the Pick-a-Brick wall. The PAB wall is where you can fill up a cup, bulk-candy style, of whatever brick they have in stock. It rules. The cups are a flat cost, so whether there are 4 bricks in there or 400, you're charged the same. Which means it's SUPER important to have a killer PAB strategy. (And of course, I've provided my tips on the next page, you're welcome.) Beyond the PAB wall, the LEGO Store has events where you can build models in-store, and they have monthly giveaways. There is also almost always a promotion going on at the stores and online, where spending a certain amount unlocks a bonus set, minifig, or other rad gift. (Pro tip: Join the VIP program! You'll earn points every time you buy, and you can use those points to save money on sets down the line.)

A PAB-ulous Strategy

The LEGO Store Pick-a-Brick (PAB) wall is a thing of beauty, but filling up a PAB cup is a lot like going to a buffet. There are loads of options, and you want to be sure to get your money's worth. Some folks get an amazing value, while others just fill up on bread and soda and don't even hit the jumbo shrimp section. I mean, HOW DO YOU SKIP THE SHRIMP?!?

You also want to enjoy yourself, so don't agonize over filling every last crevice of your cup and hurt your hand jamming extra plates into your already semi-taped lid. That's basically the buffet equivalent of getting a major tummy ache. No fun.

So consider these tips, and you'll be golden. Now I need to go find some jumbo shrimp.

1. **Fill strategically.** The little ring in the bottom is terrific for small parts like 1x1 rounds, 1x1 plates, 1x2 tiles, and other diminutive guys and gals. Fill this first.
Pro tip: There is a little stud on the PAB cup lid as well. Fill that with LEGO, too!

2. **Stack your bricks!** There are guides online of the most space-saving techniques to use depending on what parts you're getting. Personally, I love stacking and stocking up on 2x2 and 2x4 bricks at the PAB wall. Building flat disks that get slightly bigger at each level and piling them up the entire height of the cup is a great approach.

3. **Use small pieces to fill gaps.** As you stack your larger parts in the cup, there will always be little holes here and there. Fill those with LEGO.

4. **Fill your cup all the way to the top!** As long as the lid and the top of the cup make contact all the way around, you're good to go. You don't even have to be able to close it all the way. They just gotta touch. They'll even give you tape so your cup doesn't explode on your way home.

5. **Reuse your cup next time!** Not only will this save you $.50, you'll be helping cut down on waste. #reducereuse

6. **Get parts you're excited to build and play with!** Some battle-hardened LEGO vet may tell you how rare some part is and encourage you to fill up your entire cup with them. If you're not excited about having those pieces, though, it's 0% worth it. So follow your heart. Your heart knows what's up.

THE SEA CREATURE

Flying Fish, aka "The Shawk"

I've had countless chats with friends over the years about what animal I'd be, if I could be an animal. I've wanted to be strong ones like a lion, fun ones like an otter, and super chill ones like a tortoise. Being a tortoise would be pretty fantastic. You just relax, eat salads, take naps, and live for 140 years. Plus, your body is also your house. #rentcontrol

I've also dreamed about being a bird or a fish. I mean, how cool would being a shark or a hawk be? And what if you could be both?!? What if you could be a *shawk*?

Well, this build doesn't have to imagine because that's what it is. The Shawk is equally at home among the clouds and at sea. It's a mighty, noble creature, and while it may look intimidating, I have it on good authority that the Shawk doesn't eat other creatures, just peanut-butter-filled pretzels, avocados, and dark chocolate. There's apparently an organic market in the sky, or maybe underwater . . . Oh, he's actually texting me right now. I'll ask him. Ah, he has it delivered. Makes sense.

THE SEA CREATURE

EST. PIECE COUNT:
60

KEY PIECES:
6x4 wedge triple curved, inverted 6x4 wedge triple curved, 4x4 wedge triple curved, SNOT bricks, ball-and-socket joint, 1x2 plates with clips and bars, curved slopes

DIFFICULTY:

FRAGILITY:
BUILT FOR PLAY.

THE SEA CREATURE

Parts we used!

JUMPER PLATES

1x

TILES

2x

BALL AND SOCKET JOINTS

2x   2x

CLIPS & BARS

2x   1x

SLOPES

8X   4X   2X

SNOT BRICKS

2x

BOAT TILES

2x

SLOPE WEDGES

1x

1x   2x

PLATES

2x

9x   4x   1x

2x   2x

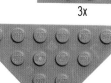

3x

2x

3x

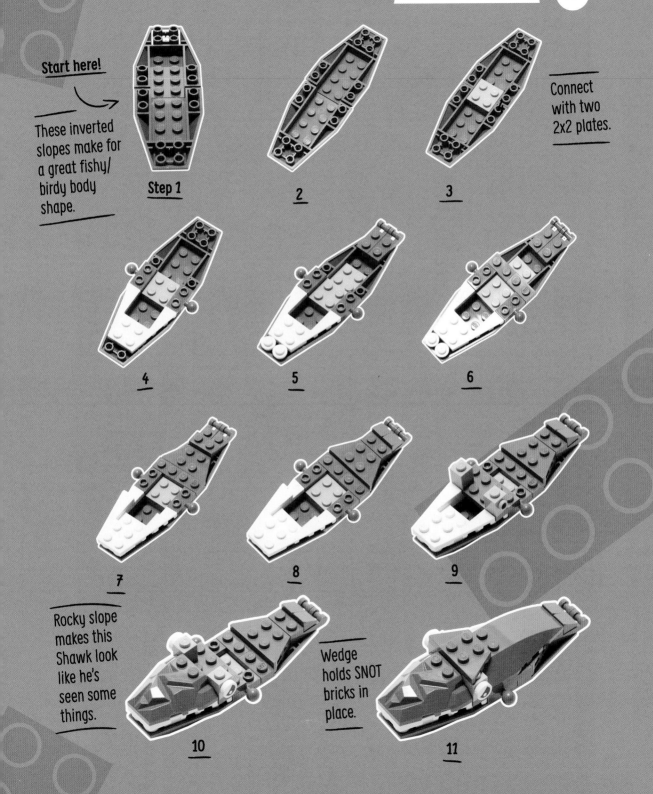

Start here!

These inverted slopes make for a great fishy/birdy body shape.

Step 1

2

3

Connect with two 2x2 plates.

4

5

6

7

Rocky slope makes this Shawk look like he's seen some things.

8

9

10

Wedge holds SNOT bricks in place.

11

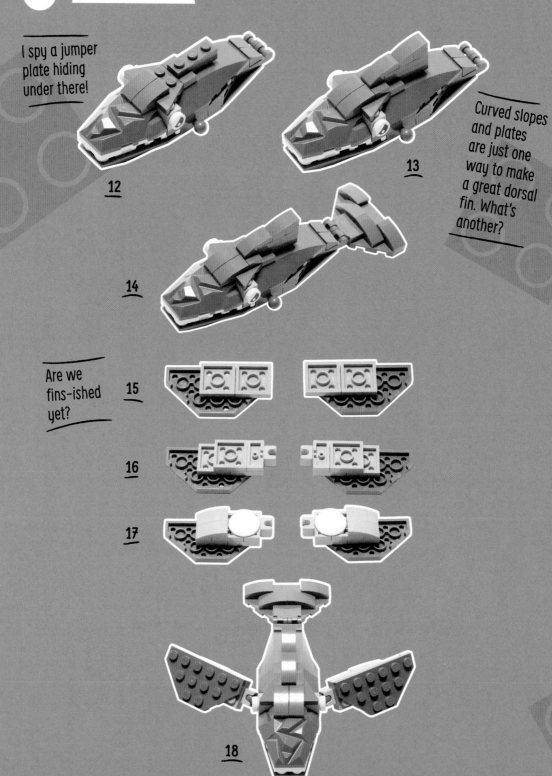

I spy a jumper plate hiding under there!

12

13

Curved slopes and plates are just one way to make a great dorsal fin. What's another?

14

Are we fins-ished yet?

15

16

17

18

Mix up the colors and **"The Shawk"** can become any type of fish you want!

REMIX IT UP

The body style can be built into a bird super easily. It's amazing how similar fins and wings are. I guess it makes sense when you think about it—swimming is a lot like flying underwater. And flying is a lot like swimming in the air. I either just blew my own mind or made the world's most obvious observation. Maybe I did both. Okay, no, my mind is blown. You could also use the same general body shape to build a sweet fighter jet, or a sweet pacifist jet. Pacifist jets can fly just as fast and do all the same maneuvers. But instead of weaponry, they have bags of tea and thoughtful note cards that they drop for people to enjoy.

The Ouchiest Pieces

I now hereby present the **7 worst pieces to step on.** Spare your bare feet the trauma and know what's coming.

The Naughty Snotty
1x1 SNOT Brick

⚡

This allover 1x1 SNOT brick is basically a land mine. No matter what direction it is, it's out to get you. The extra studs are totally awesome for building but totally awful for your footsies.

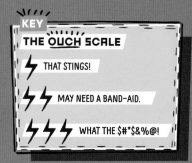

The Baddy
Rounded 2x2

⚡

The rounded 2x2 seems like maybe it wouldn't be *that* hurty, but trust me, it's a baddy. Plus it always seems to roll right under your foot and then roll away like it didn't even do anything . . . jerk.

The Scorpi-ant
Modified 1x1 Clip

⚡⚡

The design for the modified 1x1 clip was inspired by the claws of a deadly scorpion and the mouth of a bullet ant. It's a cool toy! And a painful one!

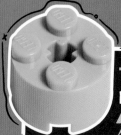

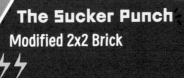

The Sucker Punch
Modified 2x2 Brick

⚡⚡

This brick has an added Technic pin, which packs a punch. Also, somehow the pin *always* sticks up. HOW?!?

WATCH YOUR TOES!
Bear traps can be anywhere!

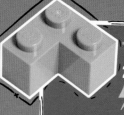

The Biter
2x2 Corner Brick

⚡⚡⚡

Oooh, extra-sharp edges! Thanks a lot, LEGO. This 2x2 corner brick resembles an open mouth, and like an open mouth, it bites.

The Bear Trap
Modified 1x2 Plate

⚡⚡

When this 1x2 modified plate is paired with its top, it makes one of the best hinges in the LEGO universe. When it is rolling solo, it is basically a bear trap.

The O.G. Brick
2x2 Brick

⚡⚡⚡

The O.G. LEGO brick has to get a shout-out, as it has been destroying feet since 1947. That's over 72 years of MAJOR OUCH!

THE HYBRID

Spider Monster Octopus

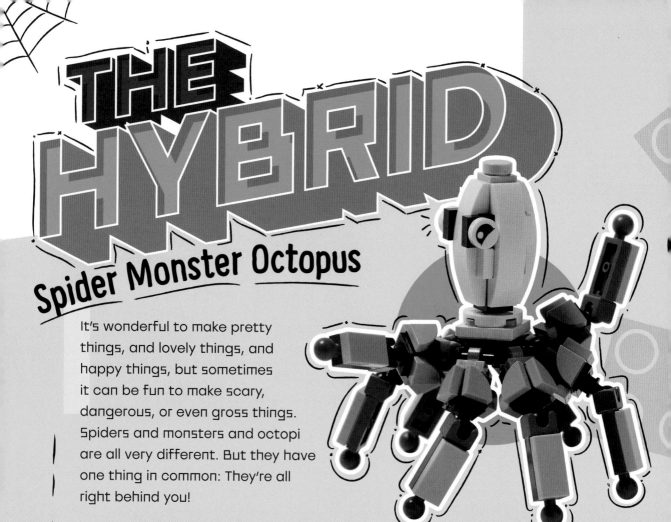

It's wonderful to make pretty things, and lovely things, and happy things, but sometimes it can be fun to make scary, dangerous, or even gross things. Spiders and monsters and octopi are all very different. But they have one thing in common: They're all right behind you!

J/K. Did you look? Did I scare you? I'm sorry. I used to be terrified of the deep end of the pool at the Jewish Community Center because I was convinced that there was a giant purple octopus that lived there. Keep in mind, this was a well-lit, indoor pool, generally filled with very loud children and very patient grandparents. But somehow, I was convinced this monster lurked in the nine-foot depths on the far end. I swam my fastest on that end of the pool. And thankfully, the violet beast never got me.

Spiders can be scary, too, but we have a strict no-kill policy in my home. In fact, I keep a small cup by the front door for our front-yard spider relocation program.

I've never actually seen a monster in real life. I've also never met anyone named Daryl, but that doesn't mean they don't exist! So whether they're out there or not, perhaps building these creatures will make them less scary for you. Let's see!

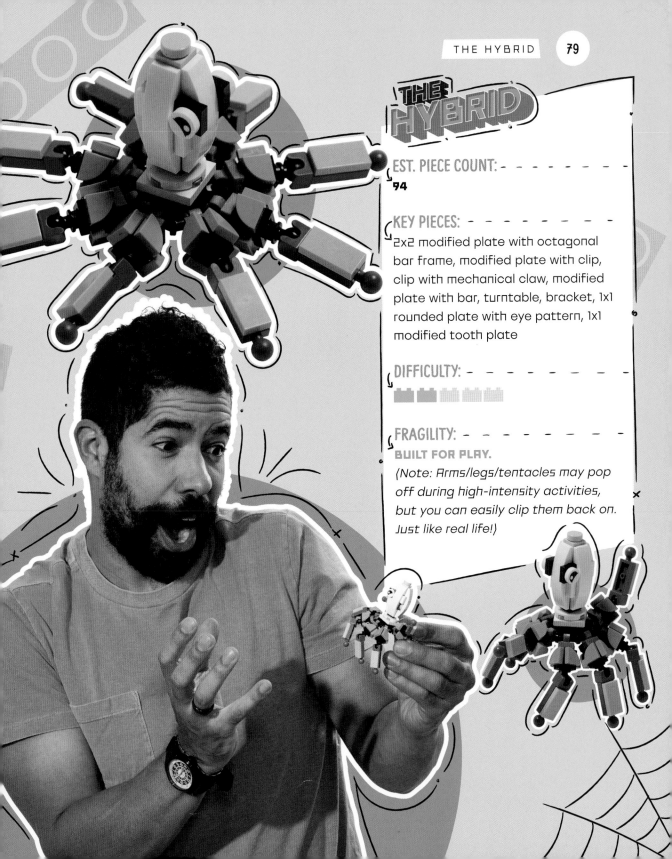

THE HYBRID

EST. PIECE COUNT:
74

KEY PIECES:
2x2 modified plate with octagonal bar frame, modified plate with clip, clip with mechanical claw, modified plate with bar, turntable, bracket, 1x1 rounded plate with eye pattern, 1x1 modified tooth plate

DIFFICULTY:

FRAGILITY:
BUILT FOR PLAY.
(Note: Arms/legs/tentacles may pop off during high-intensity activities, but you can easily clip them back on. Just like real life!)

THE HYBRID
Parts we used!

CLIPS

8x

BALL-AND-SOCKET JOINTS

8x

8x

TILES

2x

1x

8x

32x

PLATES

4x

2x

1x

1x

JUMPER PLATES

2x

TURNTABLES

1x

SNOT BRICKS

1x

10x

SPECIALTY PIECES

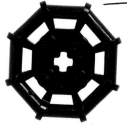

4x

1x

OCTO-BODY!

Start here! →

Place clips on all 8 sides. Any clip will do, partner!

Step 1

A SNOT brick will give you more tentacle decorating options. Woohoo, decorations!

2

3

4

Octo-legs: Assemble!

5

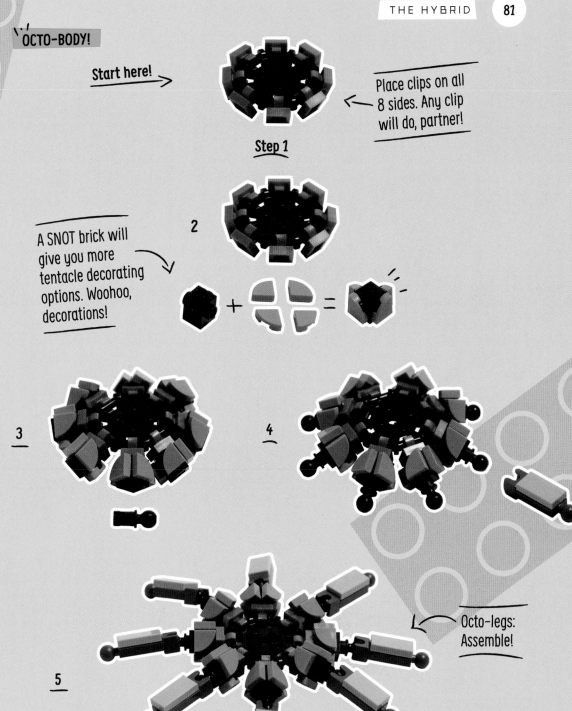

OCTO-HEAD!

6

7

8

Keep your head on a swivel, octo-friends!

Use any eye you like, or a 1x1 rounded plate.

9

10

11

Add these 4 curved slopes.

12

Front and back!

13

Left and right!

14

Head, meet body!

15

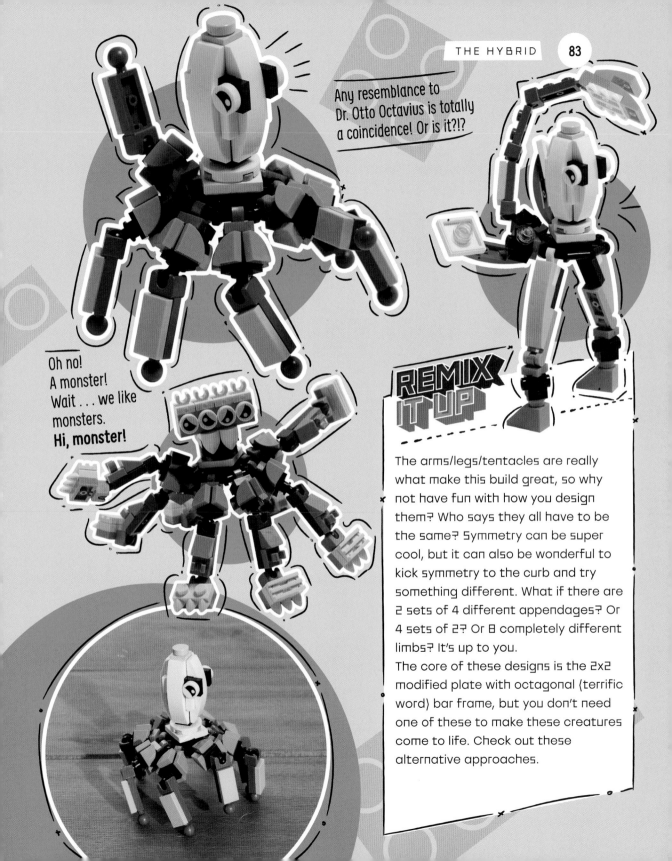

Any resemblance to Dr. Otto Octavius is totally a coincidence! Or is it?!?

Oh no!
A monster!
Wait . . . we like monsters.
Hi, monster!

REMIX IT UP

The arms/legs/tentacles are really what make this build great, so why not have fun with how you design them? Who says they all have to be the same? Symmetry can be super cool, but it can also be wonderful to kick symmetry to the curb and try something different. What if there are 2 sets of 4 different appendages? Or 4 sets of 2? Or 8 completely different limbs? It's up to you.

The core of these designs is the 2x2 modified plate with octagonal (terrific word) bar frame, but you don't need one of these to make these creatures come to life. Check out these alternative approaches.

The 6 Coolest LEGO Vehicle Sets to Take You Wherever You Wanna Go!

We all live in a colorful LEGO box!

Yellow Submarine
Theme: Ideas
Set Number: 21306
Year Released: 2016
Piece Count: 553

Why I Love It: Have you heard the Beatles? I mean, what's not to love? They're incredible songwriters, amazing musicians, and they created a world where we all live in a yellow submarine! Imagine all the fish-friends you'd make. You'd also probably get pretty claustrophobic, seasick, and stir-crazy. Now that I think about it, living in a submarine sounds like a borderline-nightmare scenario, but you don't have to live in this one! You can just take it on awesome Beatle-y adventures, explore the deep sea, and visit an octopus's garden in the shade. Plus, the build itself is super cool. Even the box rocks! It's incredibly faithful to the original shape, color, and overall design of the yellow submarine from the film. The set comes with all 4 Beatles minifigs and the wonderfully bizarre Jeremy Hillary Boob, Ph.D. (yes, that is his name).

Do I Own It? Yes! I have 2 of these stashed in my closet of "LEGO sets I think will be worth something one day."

Samurai VXL

Theme: Ninjago
Set Number: 70625
Year Released: 2017
Piece Count: 428

Why I Love It: This build is awesome! Not only does the finished product look amazing, it is super fun to build and play with. The wheels are huge, and the VXL rolls great on hard flooring or carpet. I don't know what the speed limit is in your house, but this puppy just may get you some speeding tickets. This build also incorporates an ingenious steering mechanism where the front wheels, cockpit, and rear wheels all move together thanks to a sweet sequence of Technic elements. It's rad—you gotta check it out. I tinkered with it forever during construction because the design was so interesting. I found it very inspiring and have definitely borrowed some ideas from it. You can, too!

<u>**Do I Own It?**</u> Yes! I have built 2 of these sweet rides, and I think/hope I maybe have one still in a box somewhere.

Space Police Solar Snooper

Theme: Space Police
Set Number: 6957
Year Released: 1992
Piece Count: 255

Why I Love It: I was OBSESSED with this set when it first came out. I loved how the little ship docked on the rear of the vehicle. I loved the wide tires with tread, and I extra loved that it came with 12 of them! I loved that you could detach the rear section of the vehicle and have 2 vehicles! There were so many options! I also super dug the dark green windshields and cockpit covers. I thought how they stacked on the front of the vehicle looked amazing. I still remember building this set 25 years later, and I remember taking it on all sorts of adventures.

<u>**Do I Own It?**</u> Yup! I still do. It's been broken down and repurposed over the years, but I still have all the pieces somewhere. Now I want to build it again!

The Scuttler

Theme: *The LEGO Batman Movie*
Set Number: 70908
Year Released: 2017
Piece Count: 775

Why I Love It: If you haven't seen *The LEGO Batman Movie*, go do that right now. It's so funny. It's so sweet. It's so fun. And the sets that came from it are equally amazing. The Scuttler is definitely one of the best—it's like a weird half robotic vampire bat, half mech vehicle. It's so bizarre, but it is somehow even cooler than it is odd. It has these amazing retractable arms that are built with Technic gear racks, and you can pose the Scuttler in a wide variety of ways. It's unlike any vehicle I've ever seen before or since. It's a blast to build, and just as fun to play with. It's even fun to say!

Do I Own It? Yes! I got to build all the sets from *The LEGO Batman Movie* for some episodes of *Brick x Brick*. It was a Batman-y blast!

Skull's Eye Schooner

Theme: Pirates
Set Number: 6286
Year Released: 1993
Piece Count: 912

Why I Love It: This was the first large pirate ship I ever built. I did it all by myself, too, which felt like quite the accomplishment. The ship came with working cannons, a shark, a parrot, a monkey, and even a pirate minifig with a peg leg and hook. It was great. The sails had a string that ran through them, which felt very realistic, and there was a little pulley system for the anchor and treasure chest. It was the perfect ship for weaving an epic pirate tale, and many a tale were told by I. That's pirate speak for "I played with it a lot."

Do I Own It? Yep! I was a pirate man then, and I'm a pirate man now. The question is, *arrrrrrr* you? *Sea* what I did there? It's pretty *a-parrot* that was a pirate pun. And another one. I'm *hooked*. Seriously, I can't stop.

Monorail Transport System

Theme: Futuron
Set Number: 6990
Year Released: 1987
Piece Count: 731

Why I Love It: Some people say, "The future is now." Well, they're wrong. The future came in 1987, and it was spectacular. This monorail was literally the coolest thing I had ever seen when it came out. I was blown away. The design was sweet, the space station bases were so cool, and get this, friend, the monorail *actually moved*! I know! It's incredible. That feels futuristic now, and this was basically 100 years ago. The monorail track also spanned an enormous distance. I dreamed about setting it up in my basement and building all sorts of tunnels and scenes for the monorail to travel through. I saw this as more than just a single set but rather the central element I would construct a vast space landscape around. If only it was mine . . .

Do I Own It? Sadly, I do not. This was one of the many sets that got away. It was too expensive for me to get, and it was discontinued by the time I had saved enough dough for it. If we sell enough of these books though, maybe my publisher will get me one. HINT HINT. ;)

PART 2

STUFF THAT YOU DRIVE

THE FLYING MACHINE

The Helicopter

There's a lot of talk about how technology is like magic, and it is. Our phones bounce invisible signals all over the planet, and suddenly a sloth falling out of a hammock is somehow on my screen. (Don't worry, the sloth was fine.) But I feel like we've forgotten about a certain type of magic that's been around for over 80 years. We all just pretend it's totally normal and take it for granted.

I'm talking, of course, about helicopters! Honestly, HOW.DO.THEY. WORK? That's rhetorical because there is no answer. So don't even tell me you know. You don't! Nobody does. And don't pretend to be some propeller professor, aka Prof-peller, who gets it. Because that's not even an occupation. It's just a hobby, Susan!

Seriously, I don't understand how we're not all talking about helicopters all the time. Actual magic buggies are lifting up into the sky every day, and we're just like, "Oh yeah, 'cuz it has a ceiling fan on the outside, it goes up near space . . . Yeah, that checks out."

It most certainly does not! There have gotta be strings somewhere, maybe magnets, or just flat-out wizardry.

Luckily, we don't need to know how the real ones work to build a LEGO one. Let the magic commence!

THE FLYING MACHINE

EST. PIECE COUNT:
67

KEY PIECES:
2x2 turntable, 6x2x2 windscreen with handle, various plates with clips and bars, plates, 6L bar (aka antenna)

DIFFICULTY:

FRAGILITY:
BUILT FOR PLAY.

THE FLYING MACHINE — Parts we used!

SNOT BRICKS

1x   2x

SLOPES

2x   1x   2x   4x

1x   2x   6x   4x

SPECIALTY PIECES

1x   1x   1X

GRILLES

1x

TILES

1x   1x

4x

1x

JUMPER PLATES

3x   2x

PLATES

1x   1x   1x   3x   1x

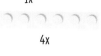

4x   5x   4x   2x   1x

TURNTABLES

1x

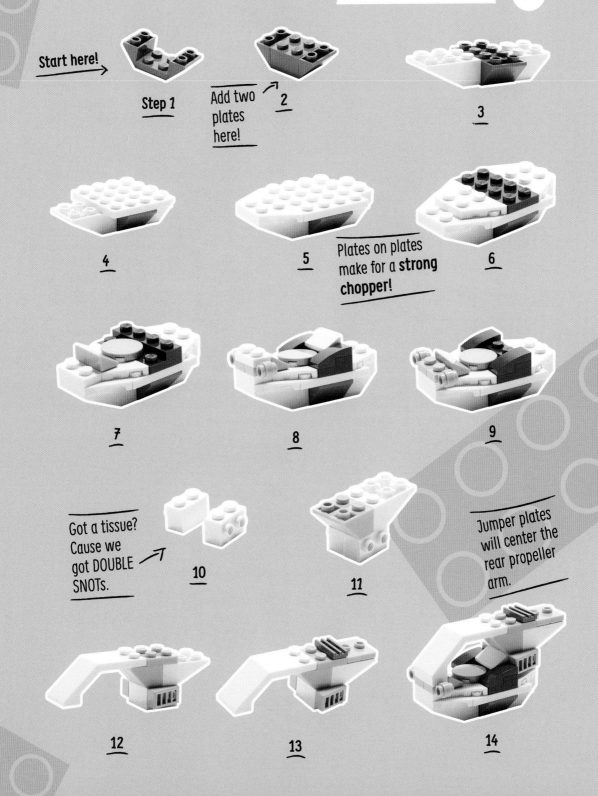

Start here! →

Step 1

Add two plates here! ↗ **2**

3

4

5

Plates on plates make for a **strong chopper!**

6

7

8

9

Got a tissue? Cause we got DOUBLE SNOTs. ↗ **10**

11

Jumper plates will center the rear propeller arm.

12

13

14

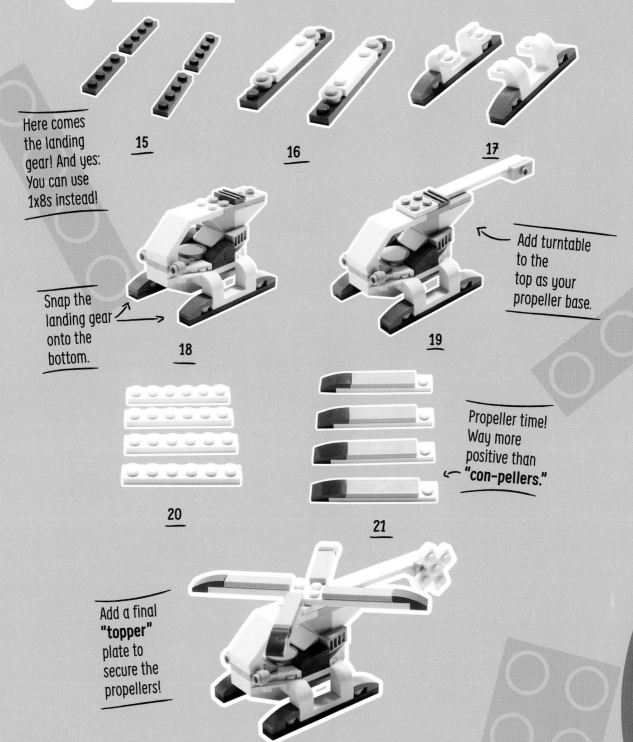

Here comes the landing gear! And yes: You can use 1x8s instead!

15

16

17

Snap the landing gear onto the bottom.

18

Add turntable to the top as your propeller base.

19

20

21

Propeller time! Way more positive than "con-pellers."

Add a final "topper" plate to secure the propellers!

22

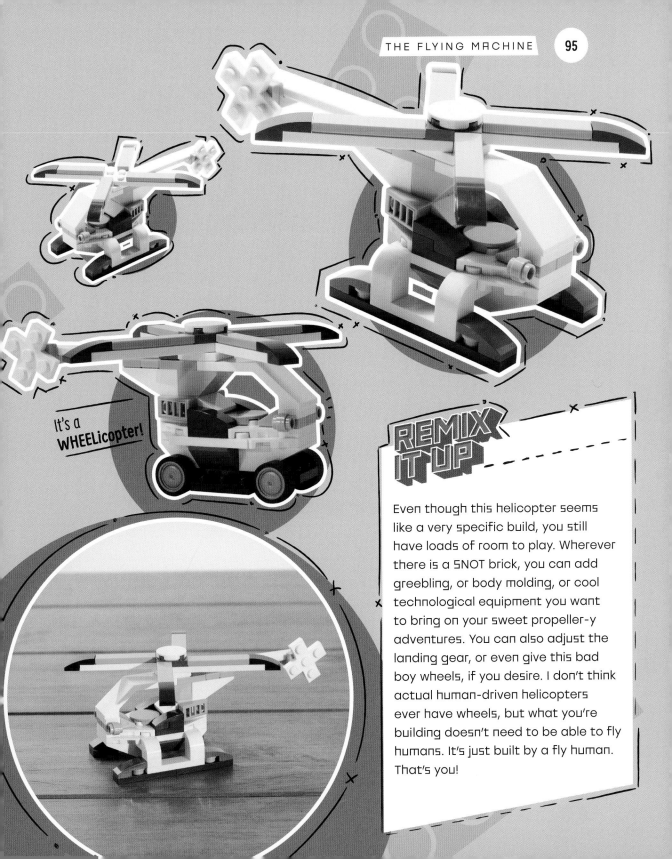

It's a **WHEELicopter!**

REMIX IT UP

Even though this helicopter seems like a very specific build, you still have loads of room to play. Wherever there is a SNOT brick, you can add greebling, or body molding, or cool technological equipment you want to bring on your sweet propeller-y adventures. You can also adjust the landing gear, or even give this bad boy wheels, if you desire. I don't think actual human-driven helicopters ever have wheels, but what you're building doesn't need to be able to fly humans. It's just built by a fly human. That's you!

Want to **Throw** Your LEGO at the Wall?

Do This Instead.

1. **Take a minute to breathe. Literally.** Here is a super helpful breathing exercise that I like to use, and it only takes 1 minute. It's a technique to slow your breathing down, which can have a natural calming effect.

   Breathe in through your nose for a count of 4. Then hold your breath for a count of 7. Finally, do a long exhale for a count of 8. The count doesn't have to be full seconds. Go at your own pace—just like building! If you do this breathing cycle 3 times, maybe, just maybe, you'll feel a teensy bit better.

2. **Take a break.** Get up, walk around your house or your room, or go outside (weather permitting) and do something else for a few minutes. You know how sometimes you get a piece of food stuck between your teeth, and you just can't get it out? You try with your tongue, then your finger with the longest nail, then your other finger, and you prod and jab, and nothing happens? Well, sometimes, when you just leave it alone for a few seconds, it kinda just wriggles out on its own. There's a lesson in there . . . somewhere.

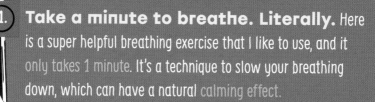

3. Ask for some help. Look, I know . . . you're an amazing builder. But all builders, amazing ones included, could use some support now and then. Even if the only person around to help is an "NLP" (Non-LEGO Person) and has built exactly as many sets as my cat. Who knows? It might be helpful! And if it's not, and their suggestion is absolutely terrible, maybe it'll make you laugh, and at the very least you'll feel better about your pre-brick-ament.

4. Throw imaginary bricks at the wall! You think I'm joking? When have you known me to joke? Oh, basically all the time? Good point. Well, this time I am semi-serious. Imagine you're holding your build in both hands and chuck that imaginary version into your wall as hard and as intensely as you can. There will be far less cleanup and way less heartache than if you threw the real thing. And as a bonus, you'll get to do some free mime practice! You may even realize that in addition to being a gifted builder, you're a rockstar mimer.

5. Speak your frustrations out loud. It doesn't matter if anyone is there or not. Sometimes it's best to do it alone, so you don't censor yourself or feel embarrassed. You can assemble a crew of your least judgmental minifigs if you'd like and just talk out what is frustrating you. Sometimes saying it out loud helps.

THE DRIVING MACHINE

Lil' Tank Turner...
(you know, 'cuz like it TURNS into stuff)

Let's just say, hypothetically, that you want a tank, and a trike speeder, and a sweet little jet that can cut through the air, go off-roading, and tear up the speedway. But you only have the space in your garage for one vehicle. Which one would you choose? Well, before you pull out all your beautiful hair and agonize over this impossible choice, what if I said you could have all three in one?!?

You'd probably say, "Adam, that's 100% impossible" and promptly call the reality police on me. Well, please don't do that! Because guess what,

señor and señora, it is possible! And that is exactly what we are about to build. So buckle up, buckaroo, it's speedy tank jet o'clock! Well, it's actually 4 minutes till speedy tank jet o'clock. So if you want to grab a quick snack, you have time.

I love love love vehicles! And I extra love love love vehicles that can travel in more than one way. Why limit your sweet little creation to one type of terrain or environment? When you have a vehicle ready to go anywhere, you can use it to tell stories that do the same.

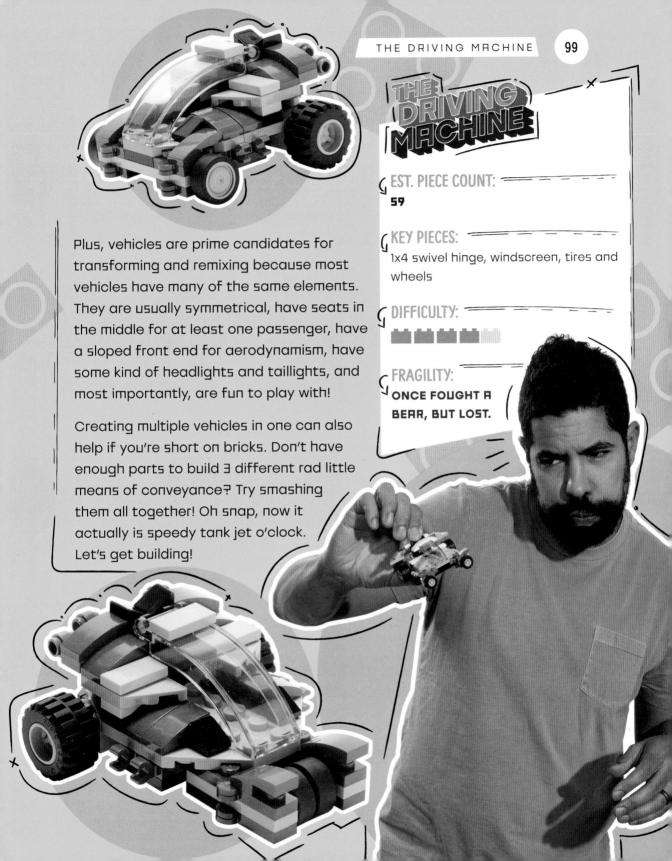

THE DRIVING MACHINE

Plus, vehicles are prime candidates for transforming and remixing because most vehicles have many of the same elements. They are usually symmetrical, have seats in the middle for at least one passenger, have a sloped front end for aerodynamism, have some kind of headlights and taillights, and most importantly, are fun to play with!

Creating multiple vehicles in one can also help if you're short on bricks. Don't have enough parts to build 3 different rad little means of conveyance? Try smashing them all together! Oh snap, now it actually is speedy tank jet o'clock. Let's get building!

EST. PIECE COUNT:
59

KEY PIECES:
1x4 swivel hinge, windscreen, tires and wheels

DIFFICULTY:

FRAGILITY:
ONCE FOUGHT A BEAR, BUT LOST.

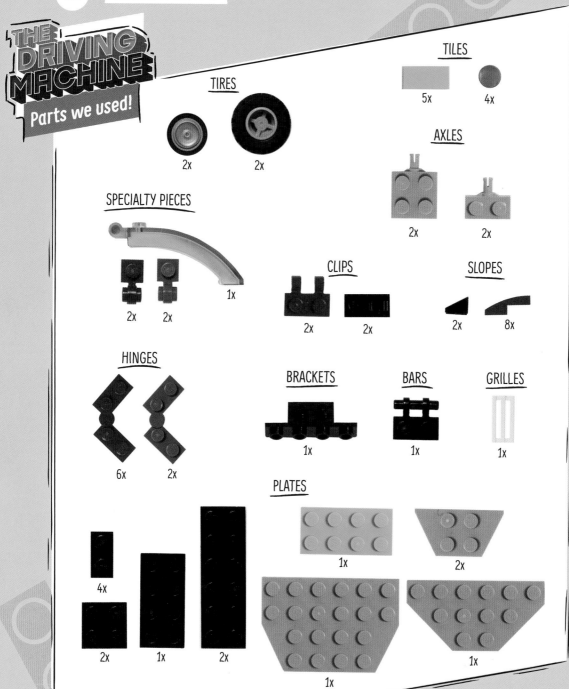

THE DRIVING MACHINE
Parts we used!

TIRES
2x
2x

TILES
5x
4x

AXLES
2x
2x

SPECIALTY PIECES
2x
2x
1x

CLIPS
2x
2x

SLOPES
2x
8x

HINGES
6x
2x

BRACKETS
1x

BARS
1x

GRILLES
1x

PLATES
4x
2x
1x
2x
1x
2x
1x
1x

THE BASE! IT'S UPSIDE-DOWN!

Start here!

Step 1

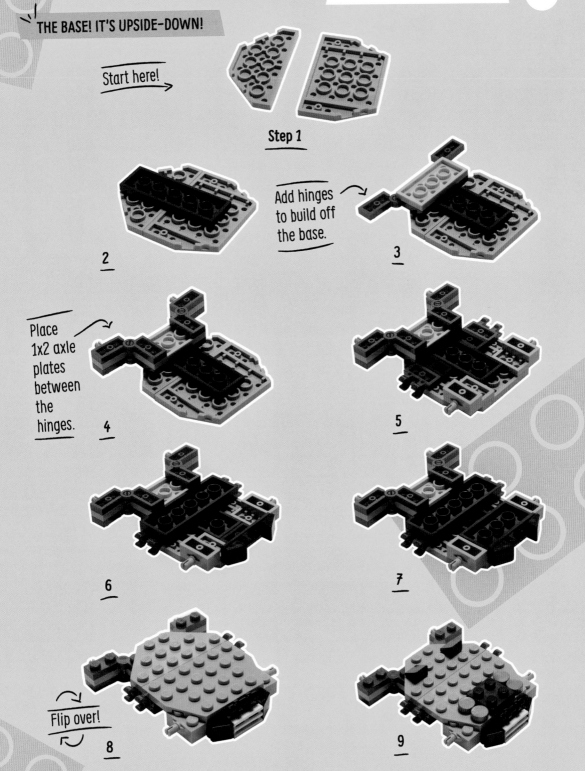

2

Add hinges to build off the base.

3

Place 1x2 axle plates between the hinges. 4

5

6

7

Flip over! 8

9

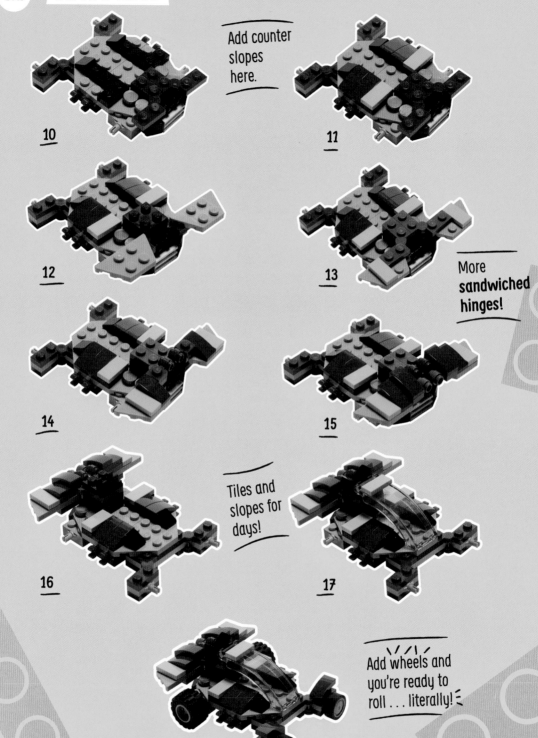

10

Add counter slopes here.

11

12

13

More **sandwiched hinges!**

14

15

16

Tiles and slopes for days!

17

18

Add wheels and you're ready to roll . . . literally!

Pick tiles and slopes of any color, and you can **personalize** your ride!

REMIX IT UP

This build has some very specific elements that fit together perfectly to create all 3 vehicles squeezed into 1. Now, this doesn't mean you can't remix it at all. You still can. But when remixing, just ensure you don't obstruct any of the parts that move, or the areas they move to.

The Coolest and Weirdest LEGO Nerd Jargon

MOC
MOC stands for "My Own Creation." This is any build you have designed and built without instructions.

PAB
PAB stands for Pick-a-Brick, and it refers to the wall at most LEGO stores where you can buy a cup and fill it with a variety of pieces. See more about the right PAB strategy on pages 68–69.

AFOL
Adult Fan of LEGO. This is the term for me! And maybe you, or your mom, or your uncle, but definitely somebody you know and probably love.

LUG
LEGO Users Group. These are officially recognized groups for AFOLs to connect with other AFOLs, share ideas, ask questions, trade bricks, and more! They are great, and there is probably one close to where you live!

BrickLink.com
This is the unofficial online marketplace for LEGO. It is huge. There are tens of thousands of sellers and millions and millions of parts, sets, and minifigs available.

SNOT

This acronym refers to any brick with a "Stud Not on Top." Although it is a bit misleading, as there is still a stud on top with these parts, but there are also additional studs on the side! There can be one, two, or four additional studs on these parts, and girl, oh girl, are they useful!

BURP

Again with the grossness! This is another yucky acronym that stands for "Big Ugly Rock Piece." BURPs were introduced in the '90s and are exactly what they sound like. They do a nice job of filling large gaps in castle walls or mountains, but they ain't pretty.

Greebling

This term may sound like another gross LEGO term, but it *isn't*. (Please applaud me for forgoing the obligatory "*it's not*" / it's snot" joke here.) Greebling is adding immense detail that doesn't actually serve a function. There are infinite greebling techniques, and it's a super fun way to enhance the visual appeal of your builds. Picture literally any spaceship you've ever seen in a movie. Now, all that cool stuff in the cockpit doesn't actually make it go to space, but it sure makes it look like it could. That's greebling!

Minifig Scale

This scale refers to the sizing that sets or MOCs are built to, so your Minifigures feel right at home. Doorways, cars, chairs, rooms, etc., accommodate minifigs' dimensions perfectly. Not all LEGO sets are built at this scale; some are smaller (e.g., Architecture series) and some are far larger (e.g., Star Wars Ultimate Collector Series).

Illegal Technique

Don't worry! The police are not on their way. Illegal techniques are just ways of connecting bricks that aren't 100% legit. This can happen when two pieces kinda fit together, but they're slightly off, or they put strain on one of the pieces involved. These techniques would never appear in an actual LEGO set but are frequently used by AFOLs in their MOCs, occasionally using SNOTs, and shared at LUG meetups. Now you understand that entire sentence!

Break the Seam

Um, Adam, why are you putting '90s surfer slang in this section? "You totally broke the seam on that gnarly barrel, bro!" It just sounds surfer-y, but it's actually quite builder-y. I promise. Breaking the seam is a technique where you stack bricks in a staggered manner so no two bricks are directly on top of each other. This lends strength and cohesion to your builds. Every brick wall in the history of brick walls gets part of its strength from breaking the seams. Just ask the Big Bad Wolf.

THE ROBOTIC MACHINE

Robot Freddie

Can you imagine a dance move so electric they named a machine after it? Well, that's what happened. Yes, that's how we got robots. Ignore all other Internet sources or encyclopedia-related references, and just trust me. Robots are named after the dance. But here's what is so great: You don't have to be the best dancer in Kentucky to boogie with this fun little robo-friend. All you need are some bricks and some tricks, and the book that you're currently reading. And you know what, you brilliant banana? You have all those things!

Also, I believe that the coming robo-pocalypse can absolutely be stopped if we build enough fun robots that actually like their jobs and want to be friends with us. That way, when your vacuum, alarm clock, coffee maker, and other boring-job-having robots try to take over the world, they can just come party with our fun robots instead. See? Problem solved. YOU'RE WELCOME, HUMAN RACE.

THE ROBOTIC MACHINE

EST. PIECE COUNT: _____
78

KEY PIECES: _____
Modified plates with clips, modified plates with bars, wheels, turntables, modified 1x1 plate with sideways stud

DIFFICULTY: _____

FRAGILITY: _____
JUST DON'T DO KARATE ON IT.

THE ROBOTIC MACHINE
Parts we used!

HINGES

4x 4x

SLOPES

2x 2x

1x 4x

TURNTABLES

2x

TIRES

6x 3x

TILES

2x

BOAT TILES

2x

BRACKETS

2x 1x 2x

JUMPER PLATES

2x 4x

BARS

2x 2x 1x

SPECIALTY PIECES

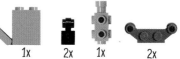

1x 2x 1x 2x

PLATES

1x 1x

2x 1x

1x

1x

1x

GRILLES

2x

2x

3x

CLIPS

2x 4x 1x 2x

Start here! →

Step 1

Start with 3 double-axle bricks.

Join the axles with ratcheted hinges.

2

3

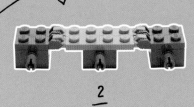

4

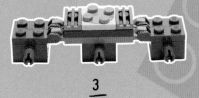

5

6

Style the lower portion like the stylish styler you are!

7

8

Add brackets and other elements to build up the middle.

9

ROBOT ARM!

10

11

12

13

Do this **twice**, por favor.

Attach the arms to the base!

14

15

16

17

This robot could use a head, yeah? Let's add one!

18

19

20

Clips and these cool handlebar pieces frame the face **super well.**

21

> Raise the roof, Mr. Roboto.

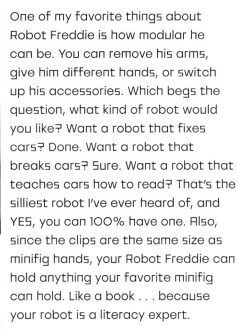

REMIX IT UP

One of my favorite things about Robot Freddie is how modular he can be. You can remove his arms, give him different hands, or switch up his accessories. Which begs the question, what kind of robot would you like? Want a robot that fixes cars? Done. Want a robot that breaks cars? Sure. Want a robot that teaches cars how to read? That's the silliest robot I've ever heard of, and YES, you can 100% have one. Also, since the clips are the same size as minifig hands, your Robot Freddie can hold anything your favorite minifig can hold. Like a book . . . because your robot is a literacy expert.

5 Reasons to Never Stop Building

Some brains are teal!

1. **Building LEGO is good for your brain.** Do you love your brain? Wanna do something nice for it? Well, I think you should. Mine is allowing me to write this sentence, and your sensational noggin is permitting you to read it. BRAIN HIGH FIVE! Since our brains do us millions of favors every hour, let's do our brain a favor and dive into some bricks. Your brain will thank you.

2. **They make LEGO sets for every imaginable interest.** Whether you're wild about Harry Potter, Star Wars, architecture, carnivals, Christmas, space, dinosaurs, animals, the future, cars, superheroes, or city scenes, there is a LEGO set or box of bricks for you.

3. **Building LEGO is fun!** I know this, you probably know this, but some people may forget. Maybe they think that LEGO is stressful, or complicated, or too hard to do. But please trust me when I say that literally anyone can build and have fun doing it. Hopefully by now you know that building something great doesn't mean it has to be super difficult. You can keep it simple, have a great time, and end up with a fun little creation.

4. **LEGO can help you connect with people outside of your age range.** I'm not up on all the "fire" slang, or Snap and TikTok stars, which can make me feel a million years old, but I can talk to kids and teens about LEGO and sound SO COOL! So if you're feeling like your cool meter could use a booster, stay up on what's "crack-a-lackin'" in the LEGO world, and you'll still be 100. Fo sho.

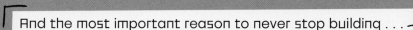

And the most important reason to never stop building . . .

5. **It's a toy you'll never outgrow.** My daughter, Plum, has some amazing toys. One of which is a little car with a working horn, steering wheel, trunk, and super fun sounds. She loves Fred Flinstone—ing it all over the house, front yard, and driveway. I can't ride in it because I'm approximately 11 times too big for it. Which is a bummer because it's awesome. Why am I telling you about my kid's sweet car? To brag about my little speedster? To make you jelly? Of course not! My point is that we literally grow out of some toys. Whether we're done playing with them or not, we simply get too big for them, and they no longer fit. THANK GOODNESS this isn't the case with LEGO. It doesn't matter how old, big, mature, fancy, or serious we get, we can always play with LEGO, and I encourage us all to do that very thing.

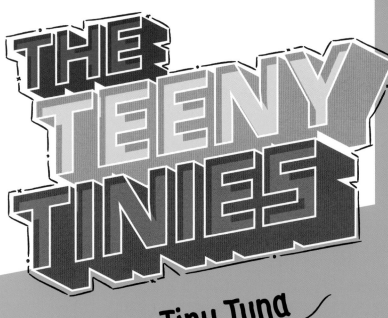

THE TEENY TINIES

Teeny Tiny Tuna

Teeny Tiny Roadster

Teeny Tiny Jet

Teeny Tiny Teddy

Ay, who you callin' Teeny?!?

One of the benefits of building smaller builds is that they can be quite strong. They're compact, and they lack many of the elements that can typically weaken a build. It's almost as if you shook a larger, weaker build until all the extra parts fell off, and these little guys were what you were left with.

So, in honor of each of these powerful pint-sized builds, I have created a powerful pint-sized poem. A haiku, to be exact. Haikus contain only 17 syllables but are still mighty pieces of art. The same can be said for these builds. While they may have more than 17 pieces, they don't have many more, and just like our friend the haiku, they are mighty.

THE HAIKUS

TEENY TINY TUNA

Shiny scales swim by
So many swift swimmers splash
School is in session

TEENY TINY ROADSTER

Engine revs heart beats
Black gloves grip steering wheel tight
Others left in dust

TEENY TINY JET

Clouds float by below
Birds fly along in a vee
Clear blue sky above

TEENY TINY TEDDY

Is it a mouse or
Maybe a sneaky cricket
Oh, it's just Teddy

THE TEENY TINIES

EST. PIECE COUNT:
Fewer than **25** per build!

KEY PIECES:
SNOT bricks, modified plates with clips and bars, 1x1 studs, jumper plates, curved slopes

DIFFICULTY:

FRAGILITY:
ONCE FOUGHT A (TINY) BEAR, BUT LOST.

Double arrows to the forearms? Why, **cupid**, whyyyyyy?!?

THE TEENY TINIES

Parts we used!

TEDDY

TILES
1x   2x
2x   2x

JUMPER PLATES
1x

BRACKETS
1x

CLIPS
2x

SLOPES
2x

SNOT BRICKS
1x   1x   2x

TEETH
1x

JET

BARS
4x
1x

TILES
1x

BOAT TILES
2x

CLIPS
2x

SLOPES
1x

SPECIALTY PIECES
2x
5x

BRACKETS
1x

PLATES
1x

JUMPER PLATES
2x

ROADSTER

TIRES
4x   4x

SLOPES
2x

BRACKETS
1x

SPECIALTY PIECES
2x

PLATES
1x   1x   1x   1x

TUNA

SLOPES
6x   2x
2x

PLATES
1x   1x
1x   1x   1x

CLIPS
2x

BARS
2x

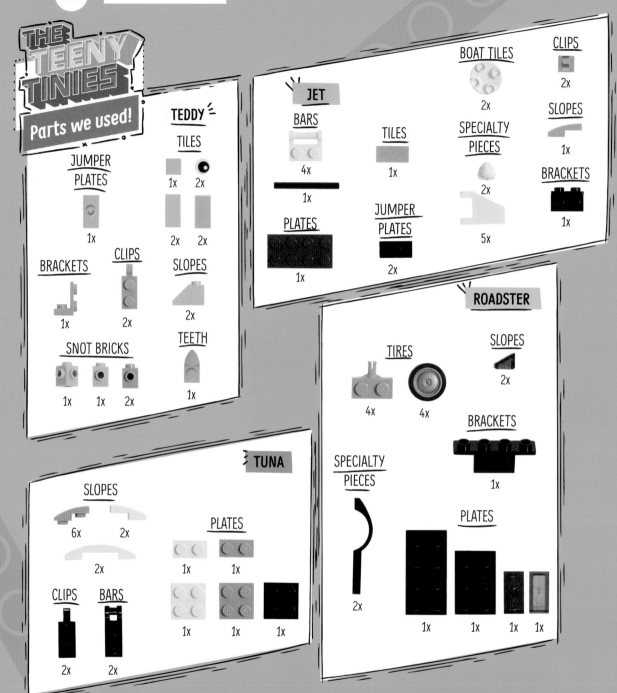

JET!

Start here! →

Step 1

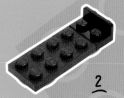

2

Add bars and wing clips on the sides.

3

4

Pose-able wings allow for cool takeoff, cruising, and landing positions.

5

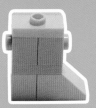

6

TEDDY!

Start here! →

Step 1

2

Position the 1x2 slopes however you'd like!

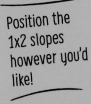

3

A 1x1 plate clip makes for a great, tiny hat!

4

ROADSTER!

Start here!

Step 1

2

3

4

Ever seen a car
this small?
Or cool?
Or both?

TUNA!

Start here!

Step 1

Clips and bars,
or hinges, work
great here!

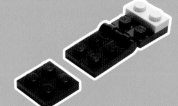

2

3

4

She swims
upstream!

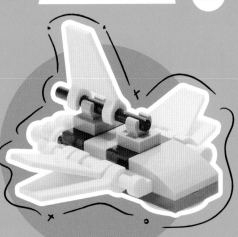

Challenge yourself to see what else you can build with fewer than 25 bricks!

REMIX IT UP

As I'm sure you know by now, you can almost *always* remix a build. These little buggers are no different. Just keep in mind that one of the things that makes these builds so fun is their simplicity and size. So limit your piece count when remixing, and see what you can do! You are in charge! It's your universe; that's why it's called a YOU-niverse. Sorry for blowing your mind.

My Fave Minifigs!

People love minifigs. I'm a people. Well, a singular person. Therefore I, too, love minifigs. And these are my 9 favorites.

Unicorn Girl (Minifigure Series 13)

I admit it. I'm a sucker for a minifig dressed up in a big, silly costume. Minifigs looked so normal when I was a kid. A big hat was as wild as they got. Now they're all over the place—it's great. Also, I love that even though Unicorn Girl is wearing a super smiley, bright, vibrant costume, she's making a face like someone just told her the world's worst dad joke. I can relate—I have both worn a big, silly costume and made the world's worst dad jokes.

Orca (*The LEGO Batman Movie* Minifigure Series)

This minifig isn't a minifig wearing an orca costume. She is an actual, full-on killer whale! Her color and detailing are awesome, and the minifig head isn't even a head at all; it's just a big tongue and hangy throat thing (or *uvula*, if you wanna be a doctor about it). How wild is that?!? Do real orcas even have uvulas? I know fish don't, but since an orca is a mammal, does it get a bonus one? Also, do orcas have tongues? Sharks don't because of all their teeth. How crazy is it that sharks are so chompy that instead of a tongue, they just have more teeth. Did you think you were going to learn so much about sea-life anatomy today? Well, you just did.

Purple Crayon Guy
(The LEGO Movie 2 Minifigure Series)

Purple is my favorite color, and we've already established that I love love love minifigs wearing big, silly costumes. Also, there was a book I was obsessed with when I was little called *Harold and the Purple Crayon*. It's about a boy who goes on a grand adventure and creates his world as he navigates it. My kind of story!

Anything is **POSSIBLE!!!!**

Kevin Garnett (LEGO NBA Minifigure Series)

I'm from Minnesota. And in 1989, we got an NBA team called the Minnesota Timberwolves. They were very bad, but nobody cared because for the first time since 1960, when Los Angeles stole our Minneapolis Lakers, we had pro hoops in Minnesota! In 1995, we had something new to get excited about. High school phenom Kevin Garnett, or KG, joined our squad. We immediately went from joke to legit. He's my second-favorite athlete of all time, behind Jackie Robinson. I met KG when I was in high school (NO BIG DEAL), and he was beyond cool to me. He's the best, and he's a great minifig, too.

Chicken Man (Minifigure Series 9)

"Who you callin' chicken?!? Ohhh . . . because I am one? I get it." See? We're having fun! This guy looks like he loves his job. I assume he skillfully flips a sign outside a place with super yummy fried chicken sandwiches.

Bigfoot ⁚ (Minifigure Series 14)

OMG! It's Bigfoot! And this time, he's not even blurry! I know, you're probably wondering why the feet of a so-called "Bigfoot" are just regular-sized. Welp, I have the answer, but I pinky swore the Loch Ness Monster not to tell anyone. Also, look how cute his regular-sized toes are! Who knew Bigfoot regularly got pedicures?!? I did. I totally knew.

Nya Ninjago Samurai
(LEGO Dimensions Fun Pack)

I love ninjas. In fact, it was hard not to fill this entire list with Ninja Turtles minifigs, but I wanted to keep it interesting and not just pull from my favorite childhood cartoon. Nya is so cool! She has a fierce face mask, samurai helmet, the double katanas, and a sweet sword backpack, which I bet has a technical name, but I already used *uvula* in this section, so I think we're good on technical terms. Also, she can turn into a robot, or maybe she was always a robot? I'm unclear, but she is super tough, very cool, and I want her on my team.

Mad Scientist

(Minifigure Series 14)

Whoever designed this minifig should win some kind of prize. He's hysterical. This guy makes me laugh every time I see his ridiculously goofy face. I mean, is this dude really even a scientist? What science is he doing? Where did he get his degree? And what's that splattered on his shirt? You know what? I don't even want to know.

Exercise Instructor

(Minifigure Series 17)

This minifig is the '90s distilled into a 4-brick-high figure. She rocks, her outfit is amazing, and her semi-afro looks like my hair did in 2009. Also, my mom and my aunt used to go to Jazzercise all the time when I was a kid, and I remember seeing these outfits everywhere. Even as a kid I thought, wait, are you for real?

THE PHONE DOCK

Phone Chomper

An herbivore is a creature that eats only veggies, fruits, and nuts. A carnivore eats only meat. An omnivore eats everything, and then of course, there are the *mobilevores*, who only eat phones. And Chompy does just that. But worry not, my concerned phone-haver, Chompy won't destroy your phone. Chompy gains his nutrients by simply holding your phone in his mouth. Trust me, it's science.

As Chompy is gaining all that sweet, nutritious value off your little pocket computer, you can video chat hands-free, snap some amazing steady pictures, stream your favorite YouTube show (HINT HINT), or just enjoy a brief break from your phone. I promise it's safe. Chompy won't text any of your friends that embarrassing photo of the time you fell asleep in your spaghetti. And honestly, you have nothing to be embarrassed about.

I wish I had a spaghetti pillow. Pasta is a great cushion option. That's why they call it comfort food.

THE PHONE DOCK

EST. PIECE COUNT:
58

KEY PIECES:
Modified plate with shield (aka tooth plate), modified 1x2 plate with 2 clips, turntables, 4x6 plate

DIFFICULTY:

FRAGILITY:
ONCE FOUGHT A BEAR, BUT LOST.

THE PHONE DOCK
Parts we used!

PLATES

1x

2x

1x

1x

1x

1x

BRICKS

2x

3x

1x

2x

TURNTABLES

2x

TEETH

8x

JUMPER PLATES

2x

CLIPS

1x   1x

BRACKETS

2x   2x

1x

TILES

3x

2x

SLOPES

5x   5x   3x

3x   3x

THE BASE!

Start here! →

Step 1

Brackets here
will help us
add arms
later!

3

This little
bit will keep
your phone
from falling
backward.

5

More
brackets!

7

2

The pink
tiles are the
start of the
mouth!

4

6

8

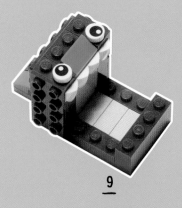

9

10

Clips hold most charging cables perfectly!

These 1x1 cheese slopes makes for rad, spiky hair.

11

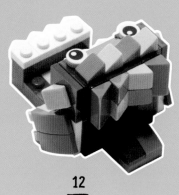

12

Now that's delicious!

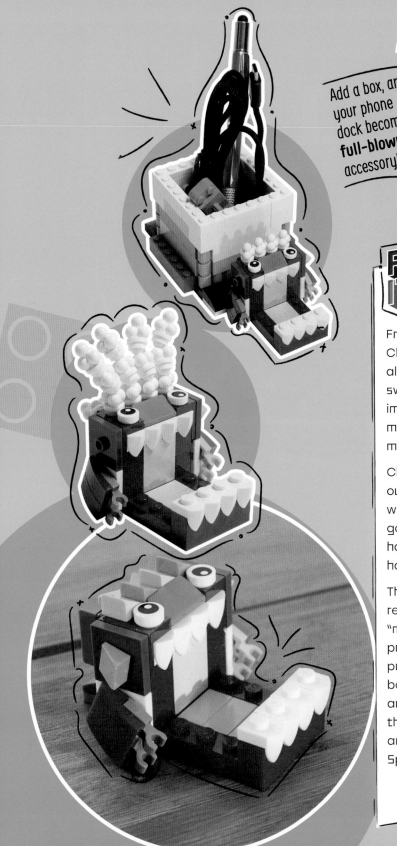

Add a box, and your phone dock becomes a **full-blown** desk accessory!

REMIX IT UP

Friends, you can do SO much with Chompy. Seriously, you can give him all sorts of different hairstyles, and switch up the nose, ears, and most importantly, the eyes, which can majorly change up Chompy's current mood.

Chompy's back can also be built out significantly. You could add a whole other container to house more goodies. You could stash your glasses, hair ties, or secret snacks, in case you have a midnight hunger attack.

The main things to remember when remixing Chompy is to keep the "mouth space" open so he can properly grip your phone. You also probably want to keep Chompy's bottom flat, so he doesn't tip over and drop your phone. Nobody wants that. Chompy doesn't need feet anyway. I mean, where is he going? Spin class? A farmer's market?

Build a **Brick Phone**

Your phone is totes lit to the max, I know. But what if you built one out of bricks? You could use it whenever you wanted to unplug a little bit. Sure, it wouldn't have all the apps or social media access or games you're used to. But it would *truly* be wireless. And you'd never have to charge it! It would never go off accidentally while you were at a play or in a movie theater.

So next time you want to head out for a walk or a beach day or urgently need to stop and get some cookies from the grocery store, consider leaving the real phone at home and bringing your brick phone with you instead. I bet you'll feel all sorts of unplugged, untethered goodness. And get this: The best part about this brick phone? No phone bill EVER! See? Now we're talking . . . just not on the brick phone. Because it's a bunch of LEGO pieces . . . it can't actually make calls.

THE CATAPULT

Snack-a-pult

YES! Actually high-five this book! ↘

Hurry! Hunger is attacking. We haven't had anything to eat in like 62 minutes and dinner isn't for like a bajillion years (aka 48 minutes). Quick, get some white cheddar puffs, grapes, popcorn, or other pint-sized "launchable" snacks and meet me at the Snack-a-pult as soon as humanly possible! Our stomachs are at stake here.

The Snack-a-pult is the perfect weapon to combat the hungers, the munchies, the peckishnesses, and even the starves. It is a terrific way to launch snacks toward your snack-devouring face part, occasionally referred to as "your mouth."

- CAUTION-CAUTION-CAUTION -

It is not recommended to launch hard or easily choke-on-able foods into your face or the face of someone you love and want to feed. It is also not recommended to launch LEGO pieces, or other hard, non-LEGO items into anyone's eyes, face, or other sensitive areas. The Snack-a-pult is only meant to help crush hunger. Please shake this photograph of my hand to ensure that you will abide by this agreement.

THE CATAPULT

EST. PIECE COUNT: _____
59

KEY PIECES: _____
Technic brick with pin, Technic brick with hole, various tiles, various plates

DIFFICULTY: _____

FRAGILITY: _____
HIT WITH BAT, REPLACE BAT.
Note: Repeated snack launchings may loosen the neck of the Snack-a-pult, so be sure to check it before initiating a hunger-crushing assault. Simply squeezing the plates and tiles of the neck back together pre-launch will do the trick.

Wait, are there dog-a-pults, too?

THE CATAPULT
Parts we used!

PLATES

1x

1x

1x

3x

1x

1x

2x

BRACKETS

2x

2x

TECHINIC BRICKS

2x

2x

TILES

3x

3x

3x

1x

PANELS

4x

4x

BRICK

2x

BOAT TILES

1x

SLOPES

2x

10x

8x

THE BASE!

Start here! →

Step 1

2

Bouillabaisse, which I think is French for **"build up the base."**

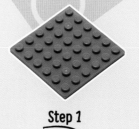

3

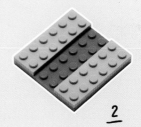

4

5

 THE CATAPULT ARM!

6

7

8

9

10

Create your **"snack pocket"** with 1x2 and 1x2 corner panels.

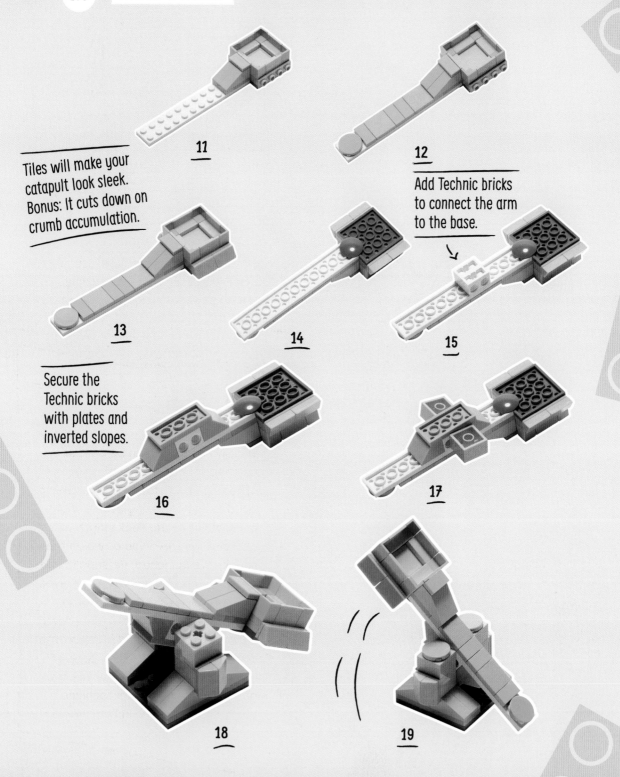

11

Tiles will make your catapult look sleek. Bonus: It cuts down on crumb accumulation.

12

Add Technic bricks to connect the arm to the base.

13

14

15

Secure the Technic bricks with plates and inverted slopes.

16

17

18

19

Play with the size and shape of your catapult and maximize the variety of snacks you can launch into your mouth!

REMIX IT UP

The Snack-a-pult can be built at a variety of different scales for different-sized snacks and different-sized hungers. Making even a slight adjustment to the neck length will also change the angle at which the snacks are launched. Personally, I like a lofty launch for my snacks. It gives me more time to make the catch. Maybe you prefer a more "line-drive" approach, you wild dude. The greater the distance between the "snack pocket" (made-up technical term) and the fulcrum (actual technical term), the loftier the launch will be.

The 9 LEGO Sets That Will Never Go out of Style

Rain sold separately!

London

Series: Architecture
Set Number: 21034
Piece Count: 468

Why I Love It: Basically all Architecture sets rock, but the skyline collection rocks especially hard. LEGO has done a bunch of great city skylines, like New York, Chicago, Las Vegas, and Paris, but London is my favorite. The Tower Bridge looks gorgeous, even at this tiny scale, and the perfect circle that is the London Eye ties the entire scene together beautifully.

Nutcracker

Series: Limited Edition
Set Number: 40254
Piece Count: 230

Why I Love It: This freebie is light on parts but big on style. It is a great decoration to bust out after Thanksgiving. I remember seeing wooden nutcrackers all over during the holiday season when I was little. I thought they were puppets and was disappointed when there was no puppet show. But this LEGO version doesn't disappoint at all. It does the opposite . . . it . . . appoints? No, that means something totally different. That means to give somebody a job. And a nutcracker has never hired me for anything. They must not be on LinkedIn.

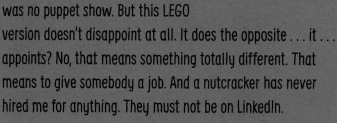

I am no lowly puppet! I am a **cracker of nuts!**

Architecture Studio

Series: Architecture
Set Number: 21050
Piece Count: 1,210

Why I Love It: This set was incredible. I'm super bummed LEGO discontinued it, but I'm super stoked I got one while they were around. It was basically just a bunch of white and clear elements, but sometimes that's all you need. The packaging was sleek, well designed, and included clear sorting trays for the parts. It also came with a lovely softcover book of inspiration and ideas.

Dinosaur Fossils

Series: Ideas
Set Number: 21320
Piece Count: 910

Why I Love It: One of my favorite things about going to the science museum when I was a tot was getting the little balsa wood models of the fossils. This LEGO set, which I don't even have yet, but VERY much want, brings that joy back, and now I can build the dinos without getting splinters!

BB-8

Series: Star Wars
Set Number: 75187
Piece Count: 1,106

Why I Love It: My wife, Stacey, is super into Star Wars. I medium am. But this build makes me like it even more. BB-8 is awesome. The attention to detail is incredible (Hello, greebling!), and the interactivity and functionality are very impressive. Plus, the fluid, lifelike movement of the semi-sphere on top is outright adorable. It is a wonderfully challenging build and incredibly fun to play with. If you have the time and funds, this is the droid you've been looking for.

Carousel

Series: Creator
Set Number: 10257
Piece Count: 2,670

Why I Love It: This set is as whimsical as it is beautiful. I hear carnival music when I see it, and I am transported back to riding the carousel as a kid. The animal seats are super cute and thoughtfully designed. The upper canopy is very realistic, and the ornate gilding around the top made me do a double take when I first saw it because I couldn't figure out if it was LEGO or not. Take this one for a *spin*. See what I did there?

Chess Set

Series: Iconic
Set Number: 40174
Piece Count: 1,450

Why I Love It: A game I love, made from my favorite building material? Yes, please! This set is great because it looks super cool, and most importantly, it's a functioning chess set! The pieces stick to their squares thanks to the centered jumper plates, so if you have to pause a game, or move the board, you're all good! All the pieces fit in the four quadrant compartments in the base of the board, and it comes with checkers pieces, too.

White knight to F3. Is that right? Did I sink your battleship?

Family House

Series: Creator
Set Number: 31012
Piece Count: 756

<u>Why I Love It</u>: This house is the perfect mix of modern and classic. Like many Creator sets, there are alternate versions to build, but the original is my favorite. It's got a light-up brick, which is always a nice bonus, and the mechanism to turn it on is clever. It also comes with a sweet little Jeep. I admit, I am a bit biased toward this build, as this was the first set I ever built with my wife. So, it gets like a million bonus points.

Furry Creatures

Series: Creator
Set Number: 31021
Piece Count: 285

<u>Why I Love It</u>: It's no secret: I am a fan of animals, and am a fan of making LEGO animals. I am a superfan of making weird, mash-up, nonexistent, mythological creatures like the "Peli-phant." Which of course is a magical beast with the giant beak and wings of a pelican, and the huge body and tusks of an elephant. Sometimes, you just wanna make a normal animal though. This set is perfect for that. The cat is my favorite, but the dog and bunny are awesome, too. Plus, it comes with a wedge of Swiss cheese. And I love cheese!

THE GAME BOARD

Ultimate Tic-Tac-Toe

How on Earth did I not call this Brick-tac-toe?

As I'm sure you probably guessed, I enjoy games! Games are the best. You never know what's going to happen, they're challenging, you get to play with your friends, and if you feel like keeping score, you may even win! But let's be real, if you're hanging out with peeps you like and having a blast, you're already winning.

My favorites are Scrabble, Connect Four, The Settlers of Catan, charades, Codenames, Jenga, tic-tac-toe, a million card games, dominoes, Clue, and 500 others. I've built a few LEGO versions of these games, and today we're going to tackle the tic-tac-toe game board. It's a great game to start with, and it's super compact, so you can take it with you everywhere you go.

Tic-tac-toe has always had a special place in my heart because when I was little, I played tic-tac-toe with Prince. Yes, you read that right. *THE* PRINCE. And no, I'm not foolin'. I PLAYED TIC-TAC-TOE WITH PRINCE. I guess that sentence could use a little bit of backstory.

As a kid, I acted. I was in some commercials, I did a bunch of plays, and I had very small parts in a few movies. One of those movies was *Graffiti Bridge*, the far lesser known but equally weird sequel to *Purple Rain*. By the way, it is FINE if you don't know these movies. I won't shame you for being young.

On set, I got to meet Prince, and I brought an autograph book because this was long before the time you had a camera on your phone to snap a selfie. He not only agreed to sign my book, but he also challenged me to a game of tic-tac-toe, or "Prince's Tic-Tac-Toe," as he called it.

We played 3 games, and he went 3 for 3. He also 100% cheated! For real! He jokingly said there were squares I could go in and squares that were reserved for him, but I was 8, so I followed his rules. He had the center square and 2 of the 4 corners, so I didn't really stand a chance, but I didn't care at all. I was playing tic-tac-toe with Prince!!! He wrote me a very sweet note, gave my mom a hug (which made her life), and I still have the book with his autograph.

Now as I've said at least 400 times in my life, "Enough about Prince; let's get back to LEGO."

THE GAME BOARD

EST. PIECE COUNT: _____
↳ **65**

KEY PIECES: _____
↳ 2x2 jumper plates, 1x1 studs in two colors, tiles, 2x2 corner bricks

DIFFICULTY: _____
↳ ■ ■ □ □ □

FRAGILITY: _____
↳ ONCE FOUGHT A BEAR, BUT LOST.

THE GAME BOARD

Parts we used!

PLATES

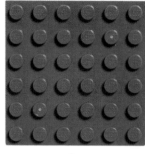

12x

JUMPER PLATES

9x

1x

BRICKS

4x

4x

4x

12x

TILES

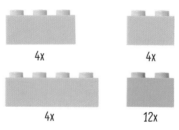

2x

4x

2x

1x

5x

5x

THE BASE!

Start here!

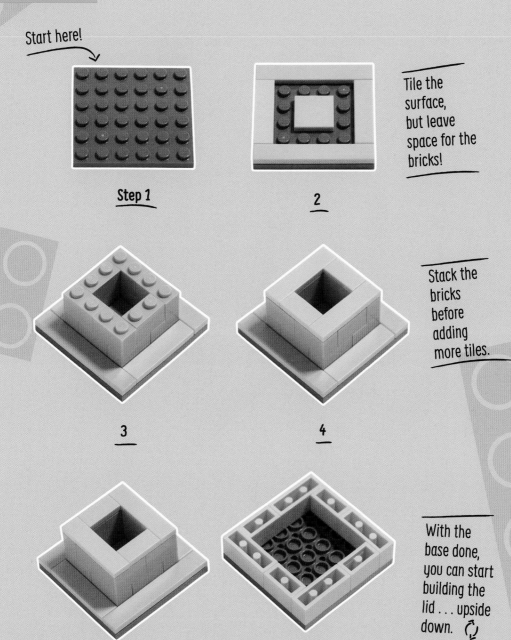

Step 1

2

Tile the surface, but leave space for the bricks!

3

4

Stack the bricks before adding more tiles.

5

With the base done, you can start building the lid . . . upside down. ↻

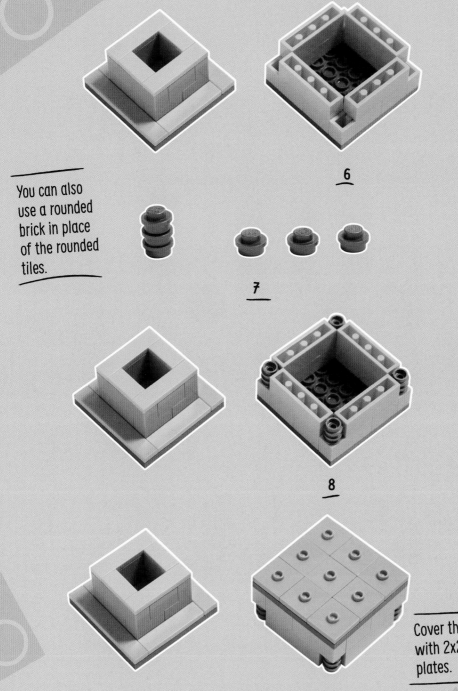

6

You can also use a rounded brick in place of the rounded tiles.

7

8

9

Cover the lid with 2x2 jumper plates.

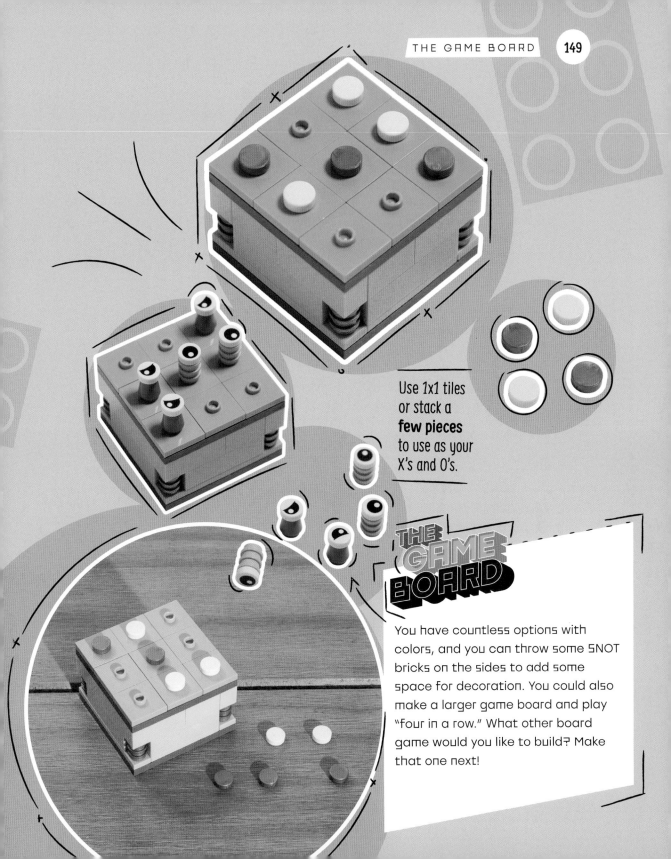

Use 1x1 tiles or stack a **few pieces** to use as your X's and O's.

THE GAME BOARD

You have countless options with colors, and you can throw some SNOT bricks on the sides to add some space for decoration. You could also make a larger game board and play "four in a row." What other board game would you like to build? Make that one next!

3 Ways to Game-ify LEGO

The Blind Build

Take a small build (ideally no more than 25 pieces) that you're familiar with and take it apart. Wasn't that fun? Not really? Oh. Well, that wasn't the game part yet! Now get a bandanna or scarf, or just use the honor system and close your eyes as you attempt to rebuild it. Seriously! No peeking! You'd only be cheating yourself. If you've got enough bricks for two builds, you could even race your friend.

GAME TWIST: GO THE COOPERATIVE ROUTE WITH A FRIEND. ONE OF YOU GETS BLINDFOLDED, AND ONE OF YOU IS RESPONSIBLE FOR GIVING DIRECTIONS. THIS METHOD CAN BE EVEN MORE CHALLENGING, BUT IT'S A TERRIFIC TEAMWORK AND COMMUNICATION EXERCISE. AND DESPITE THAT BORING DESCRIPTION, IT'S ACTUALLY FUN!

Seriously, no peeking!

Brick Stack

Stack those bricks!

Another wonderful game you can play, regardless of what bricks you have, is Brick Stack. Start with a random pile of LEGO pieces in the middle and a 2x4 brick in front of you. A 2x6, 2x8, or 2x10 brick would work, too. Just make sure that you and whoever else is playing all start with the same size.

Now take turns adding one piece at a time on top of your brick. You can build on top of the pieces you add, too. You just don't want your build to fall over or break. How many pieces can you add? What pieces are you drawing from the pile?

Brick-tionary

Grab a big pile of LEGO and jot down some reasonable nouns (person, place, thing, idea) on cards. Take turns drawing a card and building it out of the random bricks you've gathered. Now you understand why I say "reasonable." I think you'd rather take a crack at building a "moon" than "the Andromeda Galaxy," but who knows? You're smart; maybe you can build that, too.

THE COSTUME

Face Mask

Ask any artist, and they'll likely tell you that faces are one of the hardest things to draw, paint, or sketch. It makes sense. We literally look at faces all the time, so we're very used to seeing them. If one is drawn, and the proportions are a little bit askew, we notice right away and the image just looks "off."

Building faces with LEGO can be challenging, too, but we're going to do it anyway! Because that's how we roll, baby Bubba McGee! Can I call you baby Bubba McGee? Thanks!

Now there are obviously LEGO bricks that are specific to making faces, like eyeballs, bricks with printed smiles on them, teeth, and more, but we are not going to use any of these here. We're just going to use bricks,

plates, wedges, slopes, and the very important artistic element of negative space—the space left over not filled in by bricks.

When making a mask or face, considering negative space is key. With these masks, we're not going to build eyes or a nose or a mouth. We're going to build around those things, and leave them open in order to reveal their shape. It's a lot like carving a jack-o'-lantern. You remove bits until you see the image. May sound tricky, but I got your back.

THE COSTUME

EST. PIECE COUNT:
↳ 76

KEY PIECES:
↳ Cheese wedges, various plates, slopes, inverted slopes, various bricks

DIFFICULTY:

FRAGILITY:
BUILT FOR PLAY.

Don't be scared . . . it's just me!

Parts we used!

SLOPES

30x

BRICKS

2x   11x   4x

PLATES

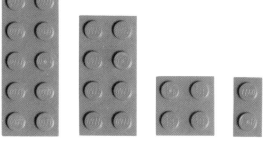

5x   6x   6x   12x

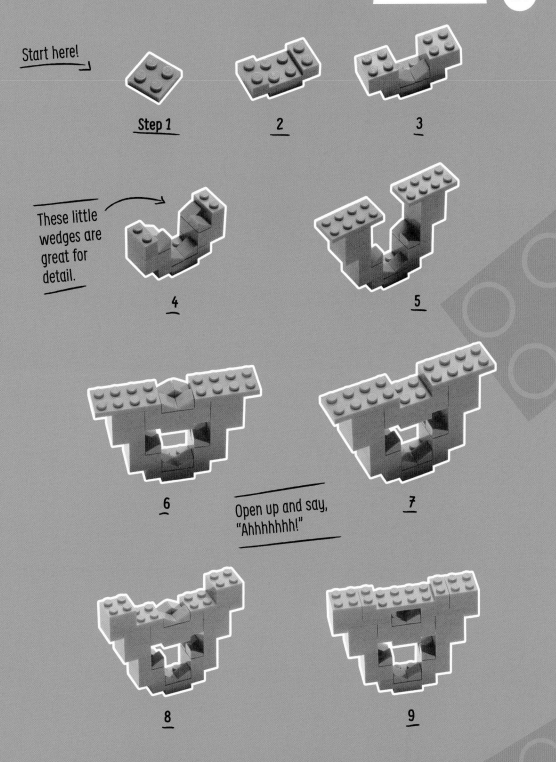

Start here!

Step 1

2

3

These little wedges are great for detail.

4

5

6

Open up and say, "Ahhhhhhh!"

7

8

9

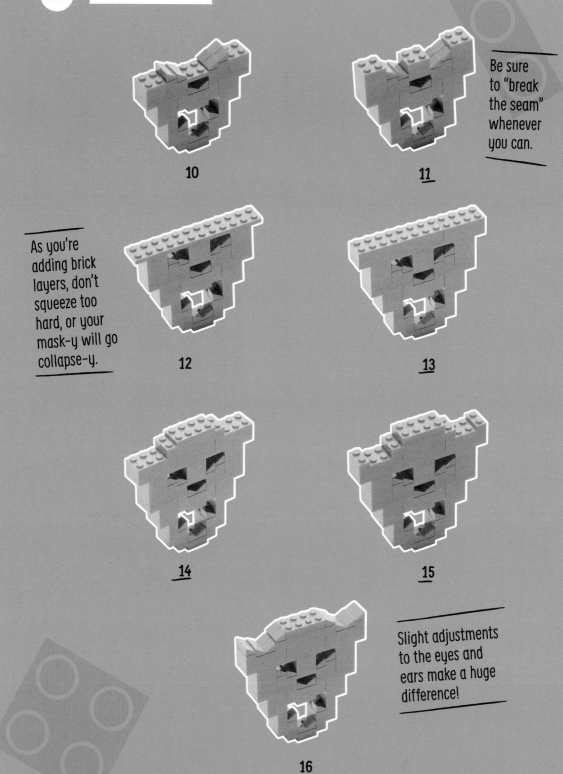

10

11

Be sure to "break the seam" whenever you can.

As you're adding brick layers, don't squeeze too hard, or your mask-y will go collapse-y.

12

13

14

15

Slight adjustments to the eyes and ears make a huge difference!

16

Brick or treat!

REMIX IT UP

A slight tweak or simple reversal of direction to the slopes or cheese wedges can completely change the emotions and expressions of your mask. This way, you don't need a different mask for every mood. Otherwise, you'd need a lot of masks! You can add more detail with SNOT bricks, play with texture beyond just having a flat front, and so much more. This is only the beginning of you making many a beautiful face with LEGO.

Self-Portrait Challenge

By now, you have accumulated some very handy building tricks, and it is time to celebrate with a picture . . . of yourself . . . made from LEGO. That's right! I am challenging you to create a self-portrait out of LEGO!

It can be 2D or 3D. That's totally up to you. And it can be your whole body, or just your fantastic face. Also totally up to you.

Sounds like a delicious piece of cake, right? Well, here is the twist, my dessert-lovin' amigo: **You may ONLY use as many pieces as you are years old!**

I want to see what you **11-year-olds** can do with just **11 bricks**, just as much as I want to see what you 48-year-olds can do with 4 dozen pieces!

Yes, that mohawk **chicken** is winking at you!

Here is my self-portrait. How do I look?

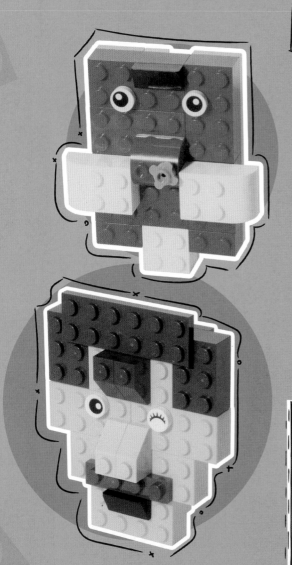

If you don't think you can manage to squeeze all of your glorious likeness into so few pieces, I'll do you this favor: You can also count your age in months. Maybe try both! Feeling really adventurous? Bust out a calculator. See how many weeks old you are, and build an amazing you with that many parts! So excited to see what you can do.

THE ARTWORK

Pattern Art

LEGO art!?! Whatchu talkin' 'bout, Adam? You may not have this reaction because you're an open, awesome genius, but not long ago, this was basically everyone's reaction when I said I was making art with LEGO. Thankfully, the world has since warmed up to the idea.

For me, there are many things to like about LEGO art. For one, when you make a mistake or, as my main man Bob Ross used to call them, "happy little accidents," you can just move the pieces and build in a new direction. You can also be super bold and leave the HLAs there and see what magic comes from it!

Building with LEGO is consistent. If I want to put a 2x2 brick on both sides, I know they're going to be exactly the same. When I draw, this

isn't always the case. I might nail the first square and then start drawing the second one, only to realize this shape is more like a sad rhombus (which is a great band name, by the way). Seriously, if you start a band called Sad Rhombus, I'll 100% rap on the remixes and help with songwriting. Also I'll get a VERY emo haircut. Just know that there are very specific cookie requests in my contract, so don't skimp!

When making pattern art with LEGO, spacing is also simple. Just like how the pieces you build with are the same in size and shape, the spaces between them, or "negative space," are also consistent. For someone like me, who likes balance and symmetry, this is a tremendous benefit.

You can easily play with elements like depth, shadow, and value. By building up as well as out, and implementing different types of pieces (e.g., bricks, plates, wedges, grilles, etc.), you can achieve a wide array of visual effects.

When you are thinking about what kind of pattern to make, there are a few things to consider. Do you want it to have many colors or be monochromatic? Do you want your pattern to be the same throughout or change? Do you want curves or just straight lines? Maybe a combination? There are no wrong answers here. Just know that each decision you make will have a significant impact on your pattern.

Starting with a simple design is wonderful because you can always add more detail as you fill it in. That's a solid place to begin, so let's get building!

THE ARTWORK

EST. PIECE COUNT:
Varies

KEY PIECES:
Totally up to you! Tiles, plates, macaroni bricks, grilles, bricks, slopes, cheese wedges are all fair game.

DIFFICULTY:

FRAGILITY:
BUILT FLAT ON A SINGLE BASEPLATE, THEY FALL IN THE "HIT WITH BAT, REPLACE BAT" BUCKET.

THE ARTWORK
Parts we used!

You'll notice that there are no part counts here. That's on purpose! LEGO art is in the eye of the builder, so follow our pattern . . . or make up your own! This is your chance to **personalize**!

TILES

PLATE

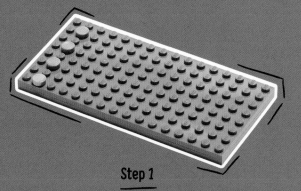

Start here! ➔

Place your first pieces, skipping a stud in between each.

Step 1

Fill in the gaps you created with your next pieces.

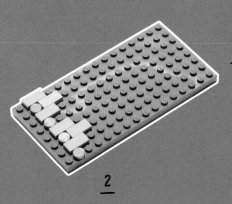

2

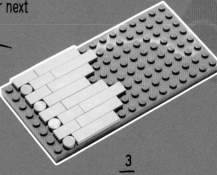

3

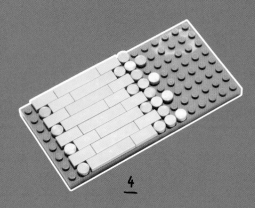

4

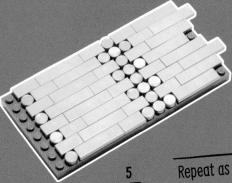

5

Repeat as much as you'd like, **you artiste, you!**

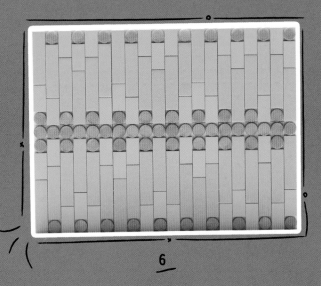

6

Playing with depth is a great way to bring new dimension to your art.

Is it zigging, or is it zagging?

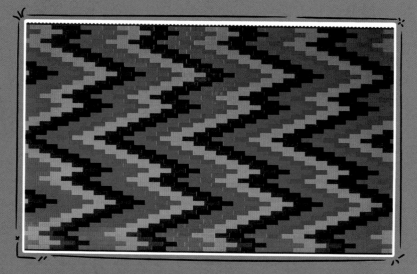

This one uses gaps in between plates.

Magnifique!

REMIX IT UP

Endless possibilities!

Make A LEGO Riddle Pictogram

Time to play a little game.

Each of the three images here represents a word or phrase that you get to decode! Don't overthink it, but you know, don't underthink it, either. Just medium think it. You can totally figure them out. I believe in you.

PUZZLE #1

Yay games! It's like a carnival, except you can actually win, it doesn't smell like corn dogs, and you don't have spend your ride money!

PUZZLE #2

PUZZLE #3

Great job! Did you get all 3? 2 out of 3? Only 1? Well, however you did, congrats! Now it's time for part two of the challenge. Oh, you didn't know this challenge was a two-parter? Well, it is, Señorita Salamander. Mind if I call you Señorita Salamander? Cool.

Time to think of your very own puzzle like these and share it with 5 friends. So grab some bricks, build your scene, snap a photo, and then email or text it to your buds. Don't do a group chat though, because if the first person to guess gets it right, it'll spoil the fun for everyone else.

Got it? Fantastic! And once they've solved yours, invite them to build their own! Then you'll have a fun little back and forth going. Like tennis, but with many, many differences. Actually, it's not like tennis at all. Never mind. I do like tennis, though.

OMG, it's **Sheldon!**

PART 4

THE

8X8

FAB

FIVE

THE PUZZLE BOX

Sheldon 1.0

If you've ever wanted to blow somebody's mind with like one hundred LEGO bricks, now you can! This Puzzle Box (aka Sheldon 1.0, aka Señor Puzzle . . . yes, the word for *puzzle* in Spanish is "puzzle") is super simple to build, and yet incredibly challenging to solve.

Just do me one favor. When you show the Puzzle Box to somebody, please, please, please give them a chance to figure it out on their own *before* you reveal the secret. It is such a treat to solve a problem on your own, and as soon as the secret is revealed, it can't be de-vealed. So even if they give up, try giving them a hint first. Everyone should have a chance to crack this "physical riddle" on their own.

Now, we all know if somebody desperately wanted to get into the secret stash of the Puzzle Box, they could simply smash it on the ground to open it. But that's what a monster would do! Certainly you're not friends with monsters, and you're not a monster yourself. Though, if you were a monster, that would be pretty cool. I mean, I didn't know monsters could even read. Let alone that they would choose my book. So, thanks, you literate monster with excellent taste! Now that I know a monster, I just have to meet a Daryl . . .

THE PUZZLE BOX

EST. PIECE COUNT:

138

KEY PIECES:

Various tiles, Technic brick with pin, Technic brick with hole

DIFFICULTY:

Note: This build isn't particularly difficult, but since it contains interlocking, movable parts, it's important to get every step right. If you misplace a piece or two, the elements won't line up properly, and you likely won't get the movement you want.

FRAGILITY:

ONCE FOUGHT A BEAR, BUT LOST.

Parts we used!

TECHNIC BRICKS

1x   1x

SLOPES

16x

TILES

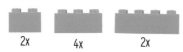

52x

BRICKS

2x   4x   2x   3x   3x

1x   7x   5x

PLATES

2x

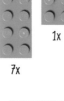

1x

7x

2x

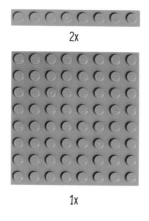

1x   10x   8x   6x

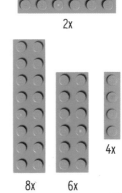

4x

Another lock?!? Man, that's secure!

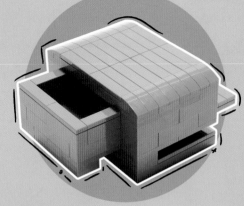

Use any combination of tiles to give your puzzle box personality!

REMIX IT UP

When we made the *Brick x Brick* episode for Puzzle Box 1.0, we were delighted to see how many people liked it and how many people built their own versions. It was awesome! People made ones just like mine; others made cool additions. Some people made great big ones that could fit another box inside it. Some people added other security features. So trust me when I say the Puzzle Box is happy to be remixed.

The primary thing to keep in mind with this and with any build with movable elements is to be sure not to block them while remixing. It's helpful to periodically test out the mechanism while remixing to ensure everything still glides, slides, and locks in place.

The Weirdest Pieces in the World

2x4 Tile with "Andrea" and Musical Notes

Piece Number: 87079pb050

Theme: Friends

What It Is: This is not a regular tile with a sticker. This is *printed* on the piece. So if your name is Andrea, you are all set. But if by some weird chance, you're one of the few people on this planet *not* named Andrea, well then I have no idea what to tell you. Maybe change your name?

Plate, Modified 12x24 with 6x6 Square Cutouts at 2 Corners and 6x6 Round Cutout

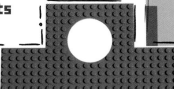

Piece Number: 18601

Theme: Dimensions

What It Is: When there are 10 words in the name of the piece, it's safe to say things are about to get weird. This base came with the LEGO Dimensions starter kit. I was super into LEGO Dimensions. This baseplate on its own, though, is quite bizarre. The shape is wild, and then there's a cup holder in the center. I'm still working on some ways to use this super rare piece. What would you do with it?

Plate, Modified 1x2 with Angular Extension and Flexible Yellow Tip

Piece Number: 61406pb01

Theme: Various

What It Is: This piece can come in handy in some builds, but that doesn't make it any less strange. It's basically a 1x2 plate with a long pokey beak on one side, but the long pokey beak has a stripe. That's not even the weirdest part. At the point of the stripe, the LEGO plastic changes into an odd flexible rubbery material that I don't think exists anywhere else in the LEGO universe. It's half rubber, half plastic, all bizarre.

Duplo Sound Effects Brick with Dark Gray Base and Castle Sounds

Piece Number: 42104cx01

Theme: Duplo

What It Is: Okay, I know it's Duplo, so this is cheating a little bit, but this piece is legitimately scary, so it deserves to be on this list. I found one of these in a random bag of garage sale LEGO years ago. Now, I thought it was way older than it actually is. This piece was introduced in 2002, which is a long time ago, but I thought it was like 1980s old. The piece has a built-in battery and speaker and makes 8 different sounds, the creepiest ones being a creaking door, a ghost howling, and a witch laughing maniacally. Yeah, "3 years and up," as in, it'll take a minimum of 36 months to get over being haunted by this piece.

Dish 2x2 with Angled Bar

Piece Number: 6919

Theme: Insectoids/Belville

What It Is: Some pieces are weird, and some have weird histories. This one is both. In the market for a disco shower head? Or are you by chance in need of an extraterrestrial snorkel? Well, this piece is for you! It could also serve as a neon fuel nozzle at the end of a futuristic gas pump. Although the dish 2x2 with angled bar may not have been used for any of those purposes. I'm not entirely sure what it did, as it mainly appeared in a few Insectoids sets back in 1998. Then, in a curious twist of fate, it was briefly brought back in a dollhouse set circa 2004. Nothing says dollhouse like alien insects!

All Bionicle Pieces Ever Made

Piece Number: Various

Theme: Bionicle

What It Is: Believe me when I say I am not being a hater. I think the Bionicle figures are terrific. Also, you know I'm obsessed with ball and socket joints, and Bionicle is built on ball and socket joints. These pieces are super funky, though! They look like they were on a meteor that collided with planet LEGO and *bam*, new alien parts emerged. I've seen incredible builds with Bionicle and have enjoyed building with them. But you can be awesome and strange . . . like the time I was at a salad bar, and there were fun-sized candy bars in a canister next to the dressing. Awesome . . . and so strange.

THE HEART

An Open Heart

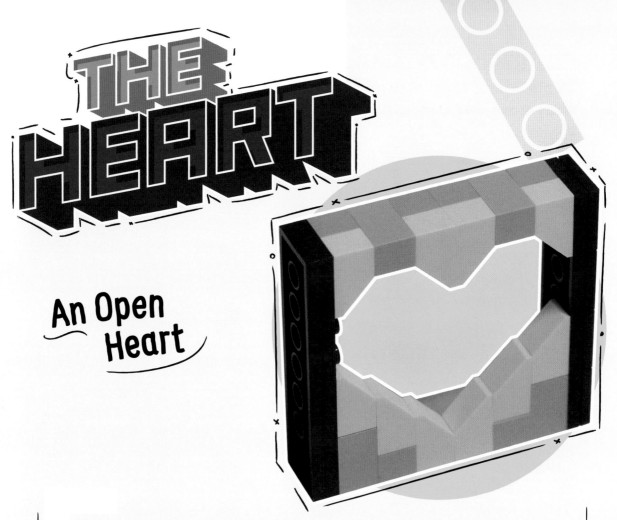

For our first-ever episode of *Brick x Brick*, we wanted to show that creativity and play can spread love. So, we literally spread the love by giving away over 50 LEGO hearts to random people all over Los Angeles. We had no idea how it was going to go. We didn't know if we would be able to find people, or if they would be open to talking to me, or if they'd be interested in getting LEGO hearts. But we tried it, and they were!

We made a few people's days, and they definitely made mine. Since then, I have built and given out hundreds more, and we've continued to spread the love (which everyone could use more of). And when I say spread the love, I don't mean hugs and smooches; I mean letting people know that you see them, acknowledge them, and appreciate their existence. This is the type of love spreading I am into.

THE HEART

EST. PIECE COUNT:

29 or so to start

KEY PIECES:

Bricks, plates, inverted sloped bricks, sloped bricks

DIFFICULTY:

FRAGILITY:

BUILT FOR PLAY.

Awwwwww
wwwwwww
wwwwwww.

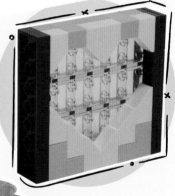

THE HEART

Parts we used!

PLATES

3x

TILES

4x

BRICKS

2x

4x

6x

SLOPES

5x   5x

This may look like the bottom, but it's actually the side!

Start here! →

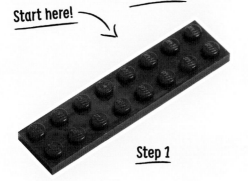

Step 1

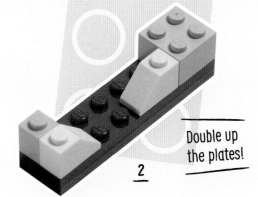

Double up the plates!

2

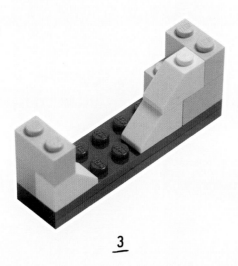

3

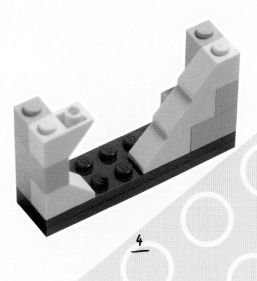

4

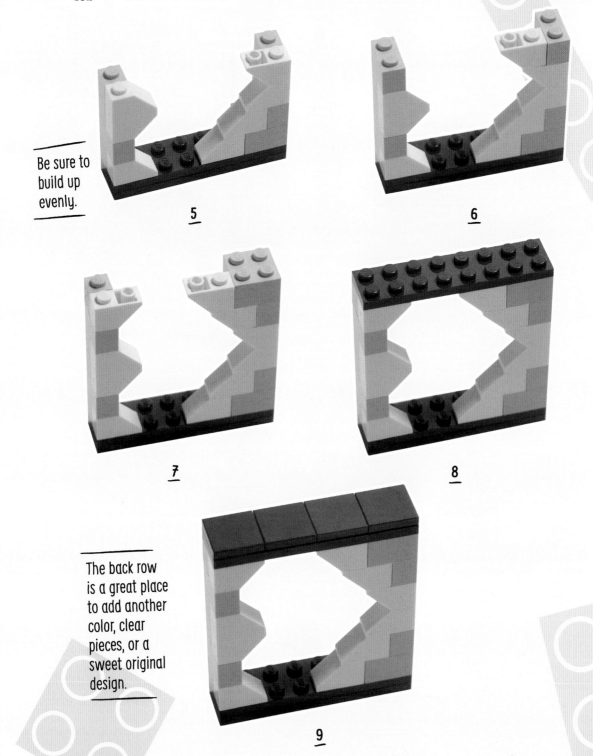

Be sure to
build up
evenly.

5

6

7

8

The back row
is a great place
to add another
color, clear
pieces, or a
sweet original
design.

9

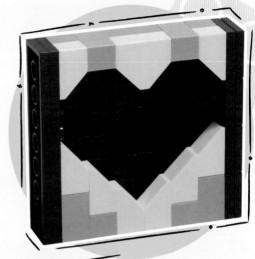

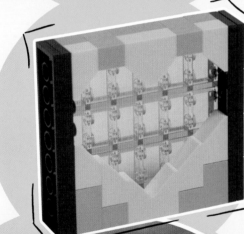

REMIX IT UP

You can remix your little heart to your little heart's content. You can even make great big hearts, or great medium hearts. Hearts of all sizes are equally important because they're all capable of love.

I know we've all seen a ton of Valentine's Day cards that would have us believe that hearts should be red or pink. But I have it on good authority from my cardiologist friends that LEGO hearts can be any color! They can even be multicolored, or striped, or houndstooth. I encourage you to make a heart that is a color or pattern that you've never even seen before—maybe that brand-new heart will generate some brand-new love.

Put LEGO on Your Wall Already! Wall-ready?!? Yeah!

Most people think of LEGO builds as going on top of a table or on a shelf or on the floor. But lucky for us, we're not most people!

It's time to get some LEGO on your wall! Now, I'm not saying *Kragle* all the LEGO you own and permanently mount it up there. That may very well be a disaster. But I am saying it's time to bring a new dimension to your building.

There are plenty of builds in this book that would look phenomenal on your wall—the heart, obviously, or the pattern art. There are other practical builds you can mount on your wall as well, like the key fob and dock and picture frame (see the next few pages for those rad builds!). Or, put your gorg new "bricksmanship" (aka LEGO letter building penmanship) on display and build a LEGO message board where you can leave notes for your family, roommates, or coworkers.

Also, if you just want to put up a baseplate, even though you don't know what you're going to build yet, that's okay, too! Once the plate is up there, I'm sure the brainstorm clouds will start rolling in. Forecast for the day: Cloudy with a chance of creativity! Ugh. That was bad. I'm shaking my head at myself right now so you don't have to. Okay, you can too. My jokes can't all be gold!

SMH, Adam.

THE KEY DOCK

Key Fob & Dock

I used to lose my keys all.the.time. Seriously. It seemed like I couldn't go a fortnight without misplacing them. And by "fortnight," I mean 2 weeks, not the online multiplayer game that is cool now, and may still be cool in the future, when you're reading this, but it will eventually, inevitably, be not cool because what *is* cool somehow always changes with time. Except, of course, for LEGO . . . that's what makes them so cool!

So where were we? Keys! Right. I used to lose my keys, and I decided to build something about it.

Now sometimes a LEGO solution is creative, but not too practical.

Like yes, of course you *could* make LEGO flip-flops. And I'd 100% give you a high five and applaud your originality and fashion sense. But they would probably be very uncomfortable, or heavy, or breakable. Or all those things. At the very least, we can agree, LEGO isn't the BEST material to make flip-flops. Believe me, I've tried.

But I think LEGO just might be the BEST material to make a key fob and dock. They're strong, they're colorful, they're customizable, and there are a number of sweet connective parts to join the fob to the dock. I could go on, but let's just build the thing already!

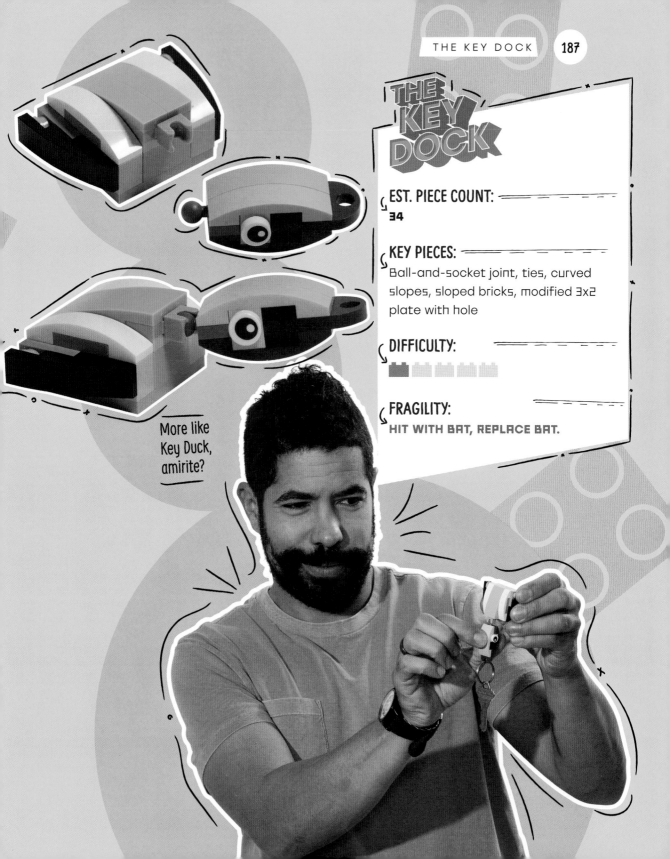

More like Key Duck, amirite?

THE KEY DOCK

EST. PIECE COUNT:
34

KEY PIECES:
Ball-and-socket joint, ties, curved slopes, sloped bricks, modified 3x2 plate with hole

DIFFICULTY:

FRAGILITY:
HIT WITH BAT, REPLACE BAT.

THE KEY DOCK

Parts we used!

PLATES

1x

1x

2x

4x

2x

BRICKS

1x

SNOT BRICKS

2x

2x

TILES

2x

BALL AND SOCKET JOINTS

1x

1x

SLOPES

2x

2x

4x

2x

4x

MODIFIED 3x2 PLATE
WITH HOLE

1x

Start here!

A 4x4 is a great base. You can go bigger if you want, but I wouldn't go smaller.

Step 1

Again, SNOT bricks help us build off the sides in cool ways.

2

3

Curved slopes take this build from good to great!

4

5

6

This large curved slope locks down our socket joint.

<u>7</u>

<u>8</u>

<u>9</u>

Slopes and inverted slopes work together for a super sleek design.

<u>10</u>

<u>11</u>

Simply fob-ulous, darling!

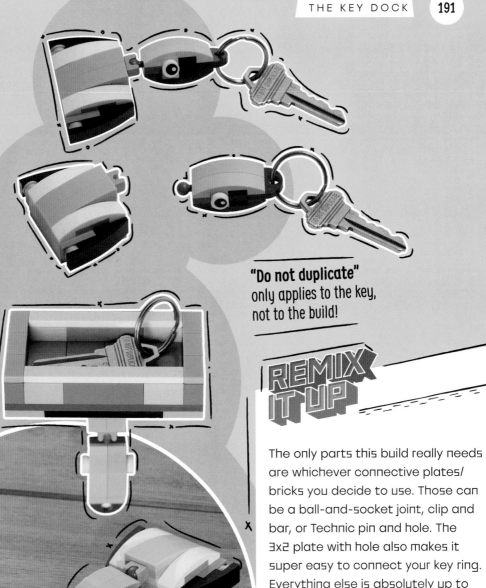

"Do not duplicate" only applies to the key, not to the build!

REMIX IT UP

The only parts this build really needs are whichever connective plates/ bricks you decide to use. Those can be a ball-and-socket joint, clip and bar, or Technic pin and hole. The 3x2 plate with hole also makes it super easy to connect your key ring. Everything else is absolutely up to you.

I happen to prefer small, smooth key fobs that don't bulk up my pockets too much. You may keep your keys in a bag, or clip them onto a strap, or just love having HUGE keys. If so, go big with yours!

Replace Something in Your House with a LEGO Version

When I first started re-tinkering with LEGO, I looked around my place and saw so many items I could replace with LEGO versions. It really opened up a whole world of building for me—I had never thought about using the toy I loved to build the things I needed. For most of my life, I had only thought of bricks as toys. This was such an exciting moment, and I want you to experience that, too.

Here's what I'd like you to do: Take a tour of your room, or entire house, or office, or wherever you spend a decent amount of time. Find something that you've been meaning to replace, or something that you just don't really like that much. Now give it away, or recycle it, or wrap it up in really nice wrapping paper and regift it to someone who would dig it.

You need a replacement for it, right? Are you going to buy one? Of course not! You are resourceful, creative, and capable, you superstar . . . you're going to build one! I hope what you got rid of wasn't, like, a dining room table, or flat-screen TV, or miniature horse, because this could take a while.

Yup, he works out.

Build in the gaps between bricks.

No, they're not hard drives. They're coasters!

THE ALPHABET

The Letters of the Alphabrick

"Writing" in LEGO is such a lovely thing to do, but it can be a little intimidating. With 26 letters and a bunch of different curves and angles, letters can be tricky to build. Once you get the hang of it, though, you will have a very handy skill up your sleeve.

We're going to start with some very basic typefaces and then pepper in some tips for when you want to step up to more difficult, decorative fonts. Hey, maybe you'll even want to tackle cursive! Ooh la la!

Lettering can also jump off baseplates entirely and enter the third dimension. 3D lettering can be amazing; it just takes some practice.

Regardless of the font or difficulty level, people get such a kick seeing their names, or a "thank you," or an "I love you" note built in LEGO. Any message in LEGO is special, unless it's a "Sorry I ate all your cookies" note. Nobody wants to get one of those . . . ever. But like, strictly hypothetically, let's say I ate all your cookies but built you a super awesome LEGO apology note. We'd still be cool, right? Like you'd probably forgive me and just buy more cookies? Cool. Cool. Good to know.

THE ALPHABET

EST. PIECE COUNT:

5+ bricks, which varies from letter to letter

KEY PIECES:

Bricks, plates, whatever pieces you want, little bean! Yes, I just called you a little bean. What are you going to do about it?

DIFFICULTY:

Note: Advanced lettering can be [■■■■■] tough.

FRAGILITY:

ALL LEVELS OF FRAGILITY.

Wonder what BxB stands for... Best Xylophone Barista? Bulky Xray Bust? Ohhhh, I got it. Blintz x Blintz! That flaky pastry show. Yup, that's it!

THE ALPHABET
Parts we used!

No part counts here! That's because each letter uses a different number of bricks.

BRICKS

No part counts here! That's because each letter uses a different number of bricks.

Leaving corners open can create a curved look.

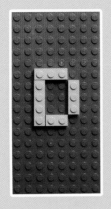

Each letter fits in a 5x5 square. This is the smallest you can go with basic bricks.

Some letters are supes easy. I'm lookin' at you, **H**!

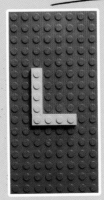

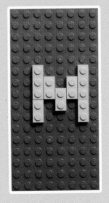

1x1s are a brick letter's **best friend.**

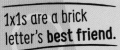

Some letters are supes tricky. I'm lookin' at you, S!

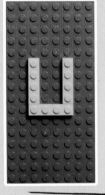

Distinguishing these two can be tricky, plus they sit right next to each other in class.

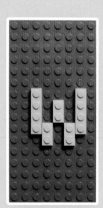

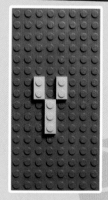

A little brick flare can really enhance the look of your letters.

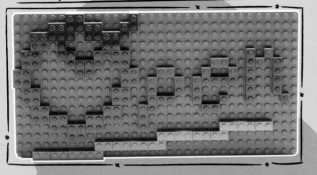

This letter is over a foot tall and weighs **8 pounds.** That's different numbers in metric!

Up for a major challenge? Make some bubble letters. They really . . . wait for it . . . **POP!**

Unlimited possibilities.

Mail Someone a LEGO Postcard

Now that you have mastered the Alphabrick, I want you to send somebody a LEGO postcard.

The message can be simple. You can just say "Hello" or "Thank you" or "I can't wait till we get to go ice fishing again, Fernanda." You can use one of these 3 template messages I thoughtfully wrote for you, or you can pick from one of the approximately infinite other things you'd like to share with someone who is important to you.

One benefit of sending someone a message is you get to feel the joy of creating it, and then they get to feel the joy of receiving it. It's like a joy sandwich. A Joywich . . . with cheese and a spicy aioli, and, of course, avocado and sprouts because they taste good and also make me feel healthy, like I'm doing something good for my body because, you know, it's a temple, and I deserve it. Yup. Like that.

If I were immortal, I'd invest in forever stamps.

It can be sent physically (you may need more than just the one stamp), or you can build it, take a sweet photo of it, and text your creation away. There is something special about actually receiving things you like in the mail, but if you can't mail it, or don't want to, a digital version is also a wonderful option.

THE PICTURE FRAME

The Chameleon Brick-ture Frame

Believe it or not, photos used to exist in places other than on your phone! I know! It's so weird. That was in the '90s when people wore lots of corduroy and flannel, and angrily mumble-sang about Seattle. But having physical photos . . . that was nice.

I'm not saying we bring back mumble-singing (besides, I think mumble-rapping has replaced it). But I AM saying we bring back printed photos. And what better way to display your photos than with your very own custom brick-ture frame?

Even if you're not into photos, or if you happen to be an invisible person or vampire who doesn't show up in photos (or wait, is that mirrors?) . . . you can always use the frame for your artwork! That way, the artwork is framed by, get this, your artwork! Whoa. Meta.

"But Unky Adam, why is it called the Chameleon Brick-ture Frame?"

Great question! You see, what I did was take the word "brick" and kinda sneakily combined it with the word "picture" because the frame is made with LEGO bricks. Get it? Pretty clever, huh?

"Yeah . . . no, um . . . we totally get that. But why is it called the Chameleon?"

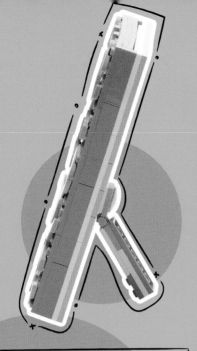

THE PICTURE FRAME

EST. PIECE COUNT:
45 for the basic frame /
96 for the version here

KEY PIECES:
Various 2x and larger plates, 2x2 turntable, ratcheted hinges, and various tiles

DIFFICULTY:

FRAGILITY:
JUST DON'T DO KARATE ON IT.

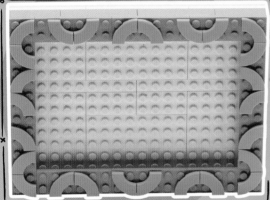

Yes, I willingly made this face.

Oh. Right. Because it is super changeable! You can adjust the frame to fit your surroundings. It can be hung on a wall, it can be displayed vertically or horizontally, it can be stood up straight, or it can be leaned back at a more relaxed angle. One thing it can't do? Eat bugs . . . as far as I know.

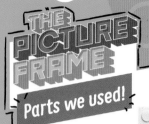

THE PICTURE FRAME
Parts we used!

PLATES

2x

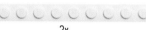

4x

2x

2x

2x

2x

15x

2x

13x

2x

2x

2x

2x

1x

BRICKS

4x

7x

1x

TILES

26x

1x

BOAT TILES

1x

TURNTABLE

1x

RATCHETED HINGE

2x   2x

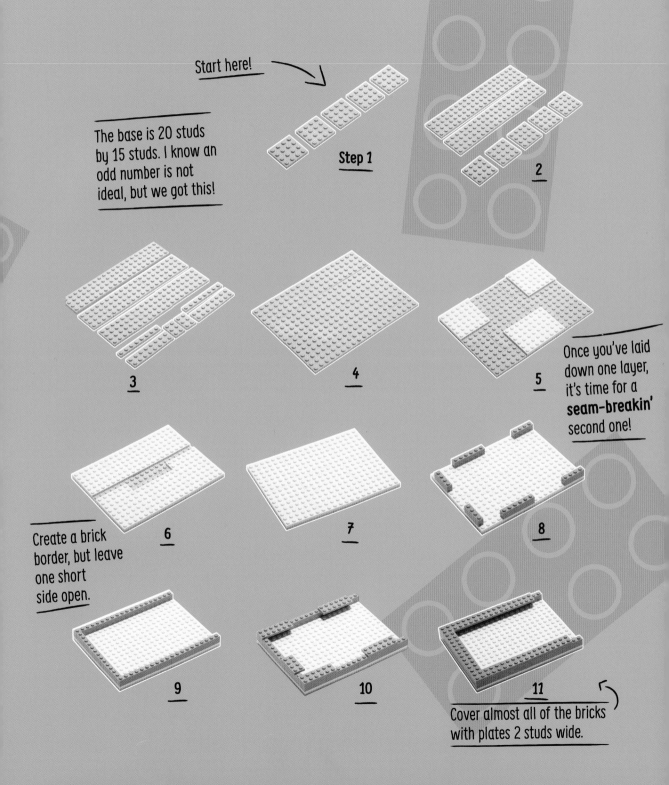

Start here!

The base is 20 studs by 15 studs. I know an odd number is not ideal, but we got this!

Step 1

2

3

4

5

Once you've laid down one layer, it's time for a **seam-breakin'** second one!

6

7

8

Create a brick border, but leave one short side open.

9

10

11

Cover almost all of the bricks with plates 2 studs wide.

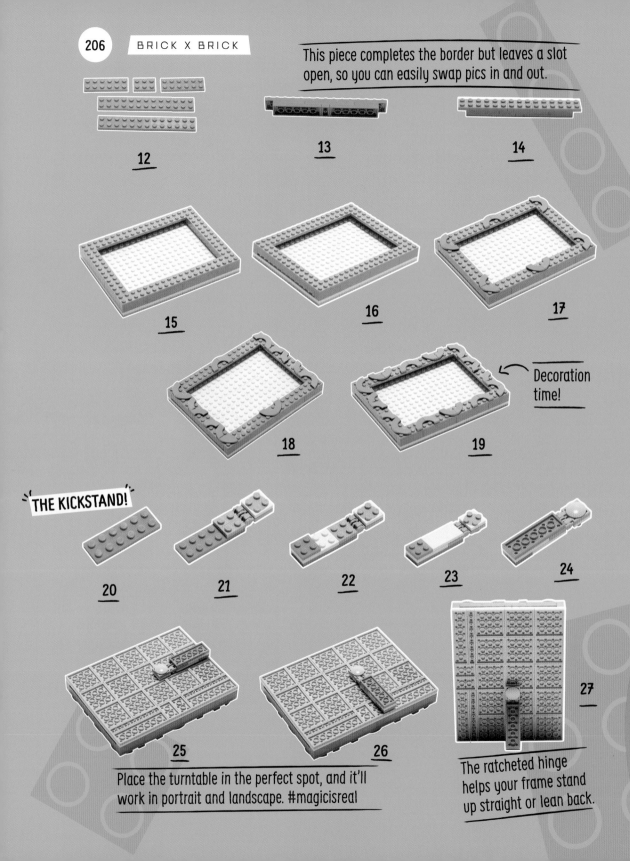

This piece completes the border but leaves a slot open, so you can easily swap pics in and out.

12

13

14

15

16

17

18

19

Decoration time!

THE KICKSTAND!

20

21

22

23

24

25

26

27

Place the turntable in the perfect spot, and it'll work in portrait and landscape. #magicisreal

The ratcheted hinge helps your frame stand up straight or lean back.

Switch it up,
play around,
keep it fresh!

REMIX IT UP

No surprise here. The brick-ture frame
loves being switched up. The border
of the frame can be customized
however you like. Why have a picture
frame for just one holiday that gets
banished to the land of "storage"
for the rest of the year? With the
Chameleon Brick-ture Frame, you can
update it throughout the seasons
and years to reflect your current
mood, interest, and style.

You can even widen the border of
the frame to give you more space
to play. Once you've mastered LEGO
lettering, you could throw some
words on there, too!

The Lessons LEGO Taught Me

You did it, you amazingly awesome human, you! You made it to the end of the book. You've created 19 masterpieces, and maybe even remixed and micro-challenged your way through a dozen or so more! You've learned some of my favorite tips, tricks, and techniques to elevate your builds and support you during your creative process. I feel like calling you a Padawan because that's a super sweet name, but since I'm teaching you, that would make me a Jedi Master. Which would be super dope, but you can't really call yourself a Jedi Master—that's like trying to give yourself a nickname. So I'll just call you Skywalker.

Before you go though, Paddy, I just wanted to share 3 more thoughts. Creating LEGO art and sharing the beauty, creativity, and joy of LEGO with fans of all ages is one of my favorite things to do in this world. But LEGO has also been one of my greatest teachers. So before you ride off into the sunrise, here are the 3 biggest things I've learned from more than 30 years of building.

1. The right pieces are out there. Just keep looking. During just about every build, I come to a point where I cannot find a certain piece. It's like if I need 12 of something, I have 11; if I need 37, I have 36. And if I just need One, I can't find that one measly part! But what I have learned is, in these instances I'm not just looking for a piece. I'm looking for a piece OR another solution. Most of the time, I find the piece. But when I don't, I find something better—another way of solving the challenge. Maintaining this flexibility—knowing that the right pieces are out there—has served me greatly in my builds and also in my life, from dating to choosing a career to now raising a kid.

2. Everything you can do now was at some point "impossible." When I was writing this book, my daughter was about 18 months old. It's amazing to see how much she has learned to do in a relatively short span of time. She walks. She nearly runs. She climbs stairs. She claps. She says "Joey" (our cat's name) 172 times a day. She waves. She dances. She does a pretty good impression of a chicken. And all of these things were "impossible" for her just a bit ago. Sometimes, when we're creating our LEGO masterpieces, we use big words like "impossible" because that's how it feels in the moment. What we mean is, "I don't know how to do this." With a little perspective, I have come to realize that what we *really* mean is, "I don't know how to do this . . . yet." I think that having the perspective and looking at all challenges (building or the things that life throws our way) with that view is key to not getting stuck. It's easy to give up if something truly is "impossible." What's the point of even trying? But if it *can* be done . . . just not *yet* . . . well then that means you're about to do something you've never done before. And that can be very exciting.

3. **A broom isn't always a broom.** Some LEGO pieces seem to be just one thing. They're introduced in a set that utilizes them in a specific manner, and they are forever labeled by that use. But what if we didn't accept that label? What if we looked at all the pieces with fresh eyes and imagined them for what they could be, not just for what they have been? There was a minifig push broom at my local LEGO Store's Pick-a-Brick wall recently. I thought it looked cool, so I got a half cup's worth. A few people asked me why I wanted so many push brooms. I didn't know the answer, so I took the brooms out and started tinkering with them. I quickly realized that a 1x2 plate or brick could be attached upside down to the bottom of the broom and be built on. I also knew that the broom was a minifig accessory, so it would fit in any clip. I was quickly building strange rocket ship boosters, and peg-legged pirate robots, and all sorts of non-broomy weirdness. In minutes, the piece that was so obviously "just a broom" had become many different things. Tinkering and using my imagination means that I can look at pieces . . . and parts of my life, even the hard ones . . . and imagine them overflowing with possibilities.

Initiate "slow clap" sequence now.

THE BRICKABULARY

Okay, so some of these terms will be super obvious to you, but I'd bet a nickel AND a button that you won't know every single one of these definitions and techniques. So dive in and learn something! If you don't, I owe you a nickel and a button. Can you Venmo people buttons?

Here goes.

Ball-and-Socket Joint

Raise your hand if you've ever used a ball and socket joint. Well, if you raised your hand, then you can raise your hand again, because guess what? Your shoulder *is* a ball and socket joint. Oh now you gotta raise your hand again, and again. Maybe you should stop now before you fall into an infinite loop of hand raising. These parts are much like your shoulder—they enable a wide range of motion in your builds, and are SO cool. They are honestly some of my faves, and we'll use them a bunch in this book. If you're making basically any animal, these pieces will help you so much. There are two sizes and a few varieties at each size.

Bar

The bar is basically BFFs with the clip. They come in a variety of styles. Together, the bar and clip make magical movements, angles, curves, and detachability. Bars can also be used to secure minifigs to your build, by serving as handles.

Boat Tile

These pieces were first used on the bottom of LEGO boat sets. Now they're used in all sorts of ways. They help smooth out the bottom of your builds and can make the bottoms of plates and bricks look way sleeker. They also allow you to use the sandwiching technique without taking up as much space as a typical plate.

Bracket

Much like the SNOT brick, these plates have studs on two sides. These pieces have a side that either sticks up or hangs down and also enables a bunch of cool, multidirectional building.

Brick

The most famous-est of all famous LEGO pieces, this is the part that people imagine when you say the word LEGO. The brick was first introduced in 1953, and even bricks from way back then will still play nice with your super duper new LEGO. Neat, huh?

Brick Separator

A super handy tool made by LEGO and included in most sets with over 200 pieces. You can also buy them separately. They are immensely helpful at taking bricks apart.

Cheese Wedges

Who knew there were 2 types of cheese wedges?!? But there are. The kind that a tiny, furry mouse nibbles on that can be super smelly if left out too long, and the LEGO kind. This piece is kind of like a slope, but not quite as tall. Imagine a 1x1 tile or a 1x2 tile where one side is higher than the other. So it's tiny, smooth, and shiny. Bonus: It doesn't smell.

Clip

These pieces can be modified plates or bricks, and come in many varieties. Clips have the same approximate dimensions of a minifig hand. That means they can hold any minifig accessory and much more! Clips work beautifully with bars and are amazing for adding movement to your build, creating angles and curves, and enabling easy detachment. I am a BIG fan of clips.

Clutch Power

Clutch power is the strength with which one LEGO element "grips" another. In other words, how strong a connection you can make between pieces. Clutch power actually varies greatly from piece to piece.

Hinge

Hinges are everywhere. The door to the room that you're currently in has probably 3 of them. Take a second and go check them out. Neat, right? LEGO hinges are a bit different than those, but they enable the same type of movement. If you want your own doors to open and close, or want wings to fold up or down on your supersonic jet, hinges will be the pieces you'll rely on.

Totally looks like a video game controller.

Inverted Slope

Think slopes, but upside down. These have larger tops than bottoms and can be used solo or in concert with slopes to make very cool angles.

Jumper Plate

A jumper plate is a plate with fewer studs on top than a typical plate. The most common are 1x2 and 2x2. Instead of having 2 studs and 4 studs on top, respectively, they only have one. This helps you center pieces and gives you the ability to move a half stud over. These are great for advanced techniques and micro builds.

Minifig

The little adorable LEGO people are called Minifigures, or minifigs for short. Minifigs come in many sets and will populate your builds, drive your trucks, fly your helicopters, and battle rap your VelociRappers. There are tens of thousands of different minifigs, and since you can mix and match the heads, arms, legs, and torsos, you can literally make millions of different combos.

Modified Plates and Bricks

These parts have a little something going on. They look mostly like regular bricks and plates, but have an extra part sticking out. Clips and bars are both examples of modified parts, and there are so many more. Modified basically means something has been done to these pieces so they can do extra stuff. These pieces help us add movement, angles, and functionality to our builds. High five for modified!

Plate

Plates may be 1/3 the height of a LEGO brick, but they are just as cool, and incredibly useful. They come in all the same dimensions as bricks and come in much larger varieties as well. Plates are crazy strong for how thin they are, and they have terrific "clutch power."

SNOT Brick

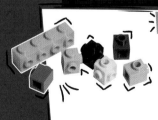

YES, it is a silly name, and YES, they are actually called this. Well, not like officially-officially, but everyone calls them this. But Adam . . . why?!? Great question! These parts are called SNOT bricks because they have at least one "Stud Not on Top." They have 1, 2, or 4 extra studs. These help you build in a multitude of different directions and do all sorts of awesome things in a very compact space. So whether you're grossed out or not, you're definitely gonna want to get your hands on some SNOTs.

Sandwiching Technique

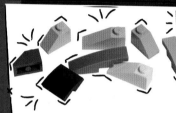

Do NOT eat!

This is a technique that is as useful as it is delicious sounding. Sandwiching plates or bricks or specialty pieces enhances the stability without affecting the appearance of the build. Basically, what you're doing is adding another layer on top, or beneath, your structure. So the assembly is stacked like a sandwich (e.g., 4x4 plate [aka bread], mirrored 1x2 brackets [aka PB&J], 4x4 plate [aka bread]).

Slope

Slopes are bricks that have larger bottoms than tops. They also have a diagonal side, which is smooth. They are terrific for creating hills, mountains, ramps, and so much more.

Studs

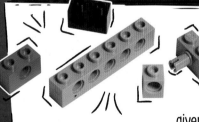

Studs are the little dots on top of most LEGO pieces. They can be solid, or have openings in the middle, which are called "open studs." Studs are also commonly called notches, dots, or bumps. They are uncommonly called "Brick Pimples," "Toppy Spots," and my personal fave, "Bumpy Malones."

Technic Brick(s)

Technic sets first came out in 1977, and they implemented more advanced techniques (hence the name) for building. They are still around today and have given us some awesome pieces that have crossed over into all types of LEGO sets. The most commonly used are the basic Technic brick with pin and Technic brick with hole. These two parts work gorgeously together and enable you to connect and disconnect different sections of your builds with ease.

Tile

Tiles are the same height as plates, but unlike plates, they do not have studs on top. They are great for giving your builds a sleek look, and they can also enable other elements to slide across them.

Tooth Plate

Modified plates do all sorts of things in the LEGO universe, but this handy little part is especially fantastic for builds that are alive. These pieces can look like teeth, claws, or toothy-claws! They come in many colors, in 1x1s, 1x2s, and they can hang down or stick out. If your build loses one, I'm not sure what "tooth plate fairy protocol" is. Maybe try putting it on your bedside table. I just wouldn't put it under your pillow. They're kinda sharp.

Turntable

These brilliant little pieces allow your build to spin freely 360 degrees! They come in 2x2 plates and 4x4 plates, and there are old 4x4 brick versions. There are other ways to create this type of movement, but these are by far the easiest. They are also super compact and have great clutch power.

Wedge

LEGO wedges come in many different shapes, styles, and even textures. A wedge is typically an angled piece that has a different number of studs on one side than the other. They can be curved, flat, or rounded. Sometimes they look like triangles, other times trapezoids, and other times like an octagon that got karate chopped in half. They can create an aerodynamic look, taper your build to a point, or just make your build look super smooth, you smoothie fan, you.

ACKNOWLEDGMENTS

A lifetime of gratitude goes out to my brilliant, beautiful wife, Stacey Storey. Thank you for the support, space, insight, and cookies. Our love fuels everything I do. Plum, Maple, Joey, and I are some very lucky mammals. Mwah. ILYAM.

MWAH!

17 PAB cups of appreciation go out to Brandi Bowles, our literary agent/ genius/possible superhero (peep her alliterative name), who believed in the book when it was just an email chain and an elevator pitch.

A jumping high five to our editor at Penguin Workshop, Renee Kelly, who helped us mine the garnets, say *adiós* to the varmints, and made this work shine its darndest. Additional daps to the rest of the tuxedo-clad Penguin squad. You fancy!

A deep bow of thanks to the sage, Shabnam Mogharabi. Your leadership and alchemical wizardry helped transform scribbles into fully formed ideas and fully formed ideas into, you know, an ACTUAL book.

26.2 props to Mick DiMaria for overseeing the third trimester of this book's gestation and helping with all the things. Your marathon-ic mentality helped us finish strong. Time to hydrate.

Cross-continental *abraços* go to design, illustration, and general visual whiz Guilherme Xavier. Your work breathed life into each page. *!Brigado, Hermano!*

An ornate serif-scripted, forearm inking of the words "THANKS HOMIE" go to photographer extraordinaire Joshua Spencer. You are even more talented than you are tatted. (And homie is SOOOOO tatted.)

A very "swooshable" spacecraft filled with fine cheeses and rare coins to Rainn Wilson for creating SoulPancake, supporting the show, the book, and lending his crafty pen to the top of this guidebook.

The widest, biggest, squeeziest, and consent-iest group hug in the history of group hugs to the cavalcade of creative and logistical unicorns at SoulPancake who magically straddle left/right brain mastery. Golriz Lucina, Dariush Brizuela-Nothaft, Chelsea Pyne, Tiffany Stelmar, Jordan Allen, Alex Findlay, Abimbola Adanritaylor. You beautiful weirdos are the best collab partners a fella could ask Siri for.

To everyone who worked on the series *Brick x Brick*: Steve Failows, Bayan Joonam, Scott Simock,

Alex Newman, Jake Menache, Cassidy Damore, Hashem Selph, Samara Pals, Kenzie Woodrow, Eric Bucklin, Fiorella Occhipinti, Jason Janocko, and more. This book wouldn't exist if it weren't for your collective energy, effort, love, and support. Jah bless.

And to the fans, super fans, and friends of the series, you dudes are the coolest, sweetest, buildiest bunch this side of the Brick-issippi. I LEGO Heart you.

So many people to thank! If this were the Oscars, that classical music would definitely be playing by now. But I just won a shiny golden man, so Mrs. Flute can wait! Typical impatient flautist . . .

Thank you to Dan Lin! You gave me one of my first jobs as a builder and invited me into the Bricksburg/Rideback/LEGO Movie/Warner Bros. family. Can't thank you enough.

Thank you Vincent Kartheiser for housing me (well, "garaging" me) when I first moved to LA. And for being the best big "frother" (brother + friend, not someone who makes milk frothy) out there.

Thank you to Hannah Blum for actively believing in my vision and supporting me as an artist and entrepreneur. Love ya, cuz.

Speaking of cousins, thank you Betsy Butwin for your legal brilliance and decade-long running jokes.

Thank you, Adam "Smiley" Poswolsky for helping me navigate the author-y waters and for never being a watery author. Pool bra!

To my Super Homies—Nate, Andy, Houston, Jack, Mark, and Ben—collectively, we have more than 140 years of friendship. That's absurd, but I did the math, and it checks out. Thank you for supporting, inspiring, and laughing with me.

Obvi I gotta thank my parents. Duh. I love you both. Thanks, Mom, for co-funding my early LEGO collection (Molly) (yes, that's an inside joke), and for filling me with belief in myself. You are relentlessly supportive always. It's amazing. Dad, thanks for being able to make things and improvise. I definitely didn't get that from Mom.

To my dear friend Levi Felix, you helped bring thoughtful play into my life, constantly "yes and"-ed me, helped me take big pauses from tech, rocked my wedding along with that booger face, Bruce, and inspired me always. Good game of sports, fish bump.

Music is a HUGE part of my routine, so big props to the musicians that provided the soundtrack to this book's creation: Brother Ali, Radiohead, Michael Kiwanuka, Run The Jewels, Dessa, Atmoshpere, John Craigie, Elder Island, The Beatles, Prince, Khruangbin, and as always, Outkast.

Finally, huge thanks go out to The LEGO Group. Thank you so much for an awesome childhood, a wonderful career, for inspiring creativity and imagination, and for empowering generation after generation. You have taught me (and continue to teach me) how to play, and live, well.

Wow—the last page. That's wild. Feels like we were just at the intro.

You made it. You did it. You're a champ!

Or maybe you're just flipping through this book at the bookstore.

Hi there! Sorry . . . I was just having a moment with the reader. We've been on this epic journey together.

Umm, I'm Adam. Also, you should consider buying this book. I worked really hard on it. I think you'll like it. I think they did. I mean, they made it this far. Have a beautiful day!

So, where was I? Yes, now that our journey together is winding down, I just want you to know how grateful I am that you chose to spend some time with me and my builds. It means so much. You've been amazing. I really hope you've gotten something valuable out of these pages, my weird jokes, strange references, and bizarre tangents.

I'm very aware of how fortunate I am. It's an absolute dream that I get to do what I do. Wonderful people like you have helped make this absurd dream a reality, so again, thank you. Thank you so much.

And please know that just because there are no more pages after this one, your journey as a builder, and as a creative force in this world, is just getting started.

Lots of love. Lots of gratitude. Lots of cookies.

—Adam

That's all Folks!

INDEX

Index compiled by
Indexing Pros
indexingpros.com

IMAGE CREDITS

All book layouts, original designs, graphics, and illustrations by
DESENHO EDITORIAL
desenhoeditorial.com

Art direction and illustrations by
GUILHERME XAVIER

Assistants:
CINTIA DE CERQUEIRA CESAR, JULIA GOUVEIA, DANIELA RIGON

Photo treatments by
INACIO TSAI

All original photographs by
JOSHUA SPENCER
joshuaspencerphoto.com

ADDITIONAL CREDITS

PAGE 8	Rainn Wilson photo by Christopher Heltai / @chrisheltai
PAGE 11	Illustration of Rainn Wilson based on photo by Jill Greenberg
PAGES 13-23	Family and personal photos courtesy Adam Ward
PAGES 26-27	Brick x Brick production stills courtesy SoulPancake
PAGE 48-49	Wooden car photo by Thomas Vogel/E+/Getty Images
	Photo of world-record LEGO bridge courtesy Land Rover
	Illustration of crane based on photo by Tatiana Shepeleva/Shutterstock.com
PAGE 55	Snakelet bracelet photo by Mick DiMaria
PAGES 66-67	Illustration of boy based on photo by Gelpi/Shutterstock.com
	Yard sale photo by Motortion Films/Shutterstock.com
	PAB wall photo © 2019 The LEGO Group. All Rights Reserved.
PAGES 84-87	Yellow Submarine box set © 2016 The LEGO Group. All Rights Reserved.
	Space Police Solar Snooper box set © 1992 The LEGO Group. All Rights Reserved.
	Skull's Eye Schooner box set photo courtesy of ThePlasticBrick.com
	The Scuttler box set © 2017 The LEGO Group. All Rights Reserved.
	Monorail Transport System box set photo courtesy of ThePlasticBrick.com
PAGE 96-97	Illustration of girl based on photo by fizkes/Shutterstock.com
	Illustration of boy posing based on photo by Jeka/Shutterstock.com
	Illustration of girl with sign based on photo by file404/Shutterstock.com
	Illustration of boy throwing based on photo by Matt Antonino/Shutterstock.com
	Illustration of boy with megaphone based on photo by Luis Molinero/Shutterstock.com
PAGE 105	Greebling photo by Mick DiMaria
PAGES 112-113	Illustration of brain based on photo by mmzgombic/Shutterstock.com
	Illustration of dinosaur based on photo by Hedzun Vasyl/Shutterstock.com
	Illustration of skyline based on photo by studiovin/Shutterstock.com
	Illustration of boy laughing based on photo by HomeArt/Shutterstock.com
	Illustration of girls on can phones based on photo by Mandy Godbehear/Shutterstock.com
	Illustration of boy on car based on photo by Zbynek Jirousek/Shutterstock.com
PAGE 122	Unicorn Girl © 2015 The LEGO Group. All Rights Reserved.
PAGE 132	LEGO cell phone photo courtesy Adam Ward
	LEGO minifigures with gadgets © 2020 The LEGO Group. All Rights Reserved.
	LEGO phone case © 2018 The LEGO Group. All Rights Reserved.
PAGES 140-143	London skyline box set © 2016 The LEGO Group. All Rights Reserved.
	BB-8 box set © 2017 The LEGO Group. All Rights Reserved.
	Carousel box set © 2017 The LEGO Group. All Rights Reserved.
	Family House box set © 2017 The LEGO Group. All Rights Reserved.
	Furry Creatures box set © 2014 The LEGO Group. All Rights Reserved.
PAGE 150	Illustration of blindfolded girl based on photo by Mike Kemp/Getty Images
PAGES 158-159	Illustration of girl taking selfie based on photo by Axel Alvarez/Shutterstock.com
	Adam self-portrait photo courtesy Adam Ward
	All other faces and character photos by Guilherme Xavier
PAGES 164-165	LEGO art remix photos courtesy Adam Ward
PAGE 166	Illustration of girl holding poster based on photo by Iryna Kalamurza/Shutterstock.com
PAGES 166-167	Illustration of heart hands based on photo by New Africa/Shutterstock.com
	Photos of Pictogram examples by Mick DiMaria
PAGE 176	Modified plate with yellow tip © 2008 The LEGO Group. All Rights Reserved.
PAGES 184-185	Illustration of girl in wheelchair based on photo by Pixel-Shot/Shutterstock.com
	Illustration of living room based on photo by Africa Studio/Shutterstock.com
	Photo of LEGO art on living room wall courtesy of Adam Ward
PAGES 192-193	Illustration of boy flexing based on photo by YuryImaging/Shutterstock.com
	Photos of LEGO accessories courtesy Adam Ward
PAGE 199	Photos of Alphabrick remixes courtesy Adam Ward
PAGES 200-201	Illustration of hands in heart shape based on photo by New Africa/Shutterstock.com
	Illustration of man with clipboard based on photo by kurhan/Shutterstock.com
	Illustration of mailbox based on photo by Dmytro Bochkov/Shutterstock.com
PAGE 207	Black and white photo frame courtesy Adam Ward
PAGE 221	Photo of 'That's All Folks' LEGO sign courtesy Adam Ward